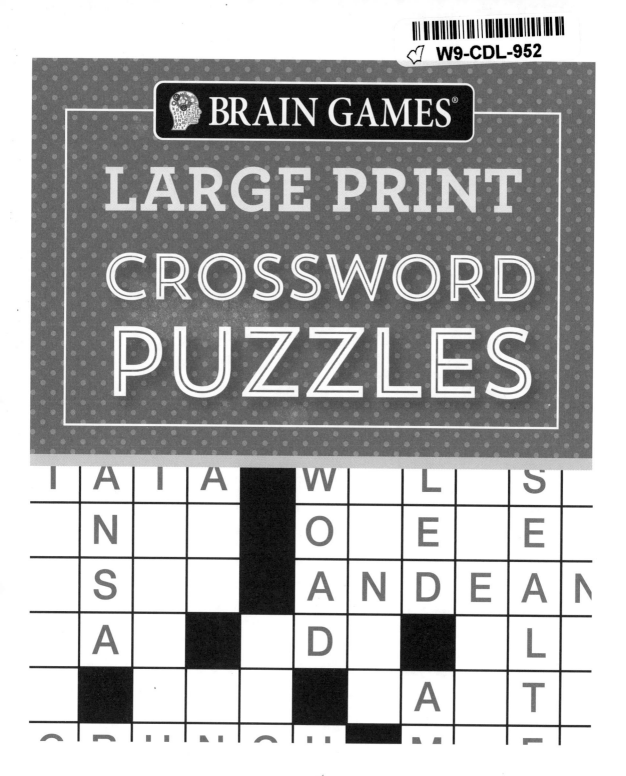

BRAIN GAMES®

LARGE PRINT

CROSSWORD PUZZLES

Publications International, Ltd.

Puzzle creators: Deb Amlen, Myles Callum, Mark Danna, Gayle Dean, Harvey Estes, Ray Hamel, Tyler Hinman, Matt Jones, Alan Olschwang, Fred Piscop, Terry Stickels, and Wayne Robert Williams

Puzzles illustrated by: Helem An, Eric Biel, Elizabeth Gerber, Pat Hagle, Robin Humer, Jen Torche, and Wendy York

Additional images: Shutterstock.com

Louis Weber, CEO
Publications International, Ltd.
8140 Lehigh Avenue
Morton Grove, IL 60053

ISBN: 978-1-64030-458-1

Manufactured in U.S.A.

8 7 6 5 4 3 2 1

FLEX YOUR BRAIN, REST YOUR EYES!

Crossword puzzles are a great way to challenge your mind and show off your knowledge of a broad range of subjects. But why does that mean your eyes have to do any heavy lifting? Let your brain do the work and give your eyes a break with *Brain Games®: Large Print Crossword Puzzles.*

This book includes more than 80 crossword puzzles to suit all interests and areas of expertise. From topics like sports and entertainment to politics and geography, there's sure to be a puzzle for everyone. With each puzzle spread across two pages, grids and clues are large and easy to read, and if you find yourself stuck on a clue, answers are conveniently located in the back.

With puns, word games, trivia, and brain-busters, get ready for a cerebral workout like none other. Sit down and get ready to reenergize with *Brain Games®: Large Print Crossword Puzzles!*

SONGS OF AMERICA

ACROSS
1. Billboard chart toppers
5. Classic creature-feature creature
9. Baseball club
12. Decide not to include
13. Civil-rights activist Guinier
14. Faerie Queene heroine
15. Annapolis institution, initially
16. Celebrity hairdresser Jose
17. Roadside lodging retreat
18. 1974 Johnny Cash song-poem
21. More compressed
22. In an inept way
23. Hand communication: Abbr.
24. Tokyo carrier, for short
25. Appliance company in Iowa
28. Gets started on
31. 2009 Miley Cyrus song
34. Bee: Prefix
35. "Beware the ___ of March!"
36. British streetcar
37. "Treasure Island" author's inits.
38. "Did You Ever ___ Dream Walking?" (1933 hit)
39. Buster Brown's bulldog
40. Casual top, casually
41. Con's stretch
42. Low bills

DOWN
1. Fifty minutes, to a psychiatrist
2. Words next to a frowny face
3. Faint coloring
4. Like backwater
5. "Gilmore Girls" co-star Alexis
6. Repair bill part
7. Scott Turow book set in Harvard
8. Warbler's watering hole
9. Play with Lincoln Logs, say
10. One year record
11. Like some barbecue sauce
19. Lamb or Bacon, e.g.
20. How Tiny Tim sang
24. Flotsam's partner
25. Away from everything else
26. Syrup sap source
27. Get up
28. Show of contempt
29. City on the Po River
30. Tribe based in Oklahoma
32. ___ fixe (obsession)
33. Iowa State's town

Answers on page 178.

NURSERY RHYMES

ACROSS

1. Big exam
6. "Small bites" snacks
11. What there is "nothin' like"
12. Davy Crockett's last stand
13. Start of a romantic nursery rhyme
15. US Army E-6
16. Airport screener's org.
17. Colorado ___, Colo.
20. Genetic info carrier
22. El Dorado's makeup
23. Antennae
27. Dopey fairgoer of nursery rhymes
29. In a romantic mood
30. Billy goat's bleat
31. Nope's counterpart
32. Aladdin's prize
33. Grade in the 70s
36. Old newspaper section, briefly
38. Merry soul of nursery rhymes
43. Fathers, to babies
44. "You are not!" rejoinder
45. Animal that sleeps upside down
46. Alternative to heels

DOWN

1. In the distance
2. Nuptial response
3. "Life Is Good" rapper
4. Sold for ___ of pottage
5. Smaller amount
6. Sourball quality
7. Pint at the pub
8. Acting role
9. Home of Iowa's Cyclones
10. Coke, for example
14. Mutually accept
17. "Slammin' Sammy" of baseball
18. Extremely proper
19. Former Dallas QB Tony
21. "Rope-a-dope" boxer
23. Thrive
24. Austen title heroine
25. Go hither and yon
26. Break sharply
28. Use a crowbar on
32. Train that makes all stops
33. New England fishes
34. Airline of Israel
35. Taro root
37. End-of-week mantra
39. "Krazy" comics feline
40. Grandma, in Germany
41. D-Day amphibian craft
42. Dawn goddess

Crossword grid (handwritten answers):

1	2	3	4	5		6	7	8	9	10
F	I	N	A	L	■	T	A	P	A	S
11 A	D	A	M	E	■	12 A	L	A	M	O
13 R	O	S	E	S	14 A	R	E	R	E	D
■	■	■	15 B	S	G	F	■	16 T	S	A
17 S	18 P	19 R	S	■	20 R	N	21 A	■	■	■
22 O	R	O	■	23 F	E	E	L	24 E	25 R	26 S
27 S	I	M	28 P	L	E	S	I	M	O	N
29 A	M	O	R	O	U	S	■	30 M	A	A
■	■	■	31 U	E	P	■	32 L	A	M	P
33 C	34 E	35 E	■	36 R	O	37 T	O	■	■	■
38 O	L	D	39 K	I	N	G	C	40 O	41 L	42 E
43 D	A	D	A	S	■	44 I	A	M	S	O
45 S	L	O		H	■	46 F	L	A	T	S

Answers on page 178.

JANE AUSTEN

ACROSS
1. Dutch town known for its pottery
6. Price of "Mansfield Park"
11. "The Nutcracker" girl
12. CSA commander
13. "RUR" playwright Karel
14. Florida's "Horse Capital of the World"
15. "Disco Duck" singer Rick
17. Dungeons & Dragons co., once
18. Expecting
22. "So love ___ leave me..." (ABBA lyric)
23. "Scooby-Doo" girl and "Chicago" role
27. Like the acid in apples
29. Authoritative decrees
30. At the summit
32. Comically outlandish
33. Indonesian volcano that erupted in 1883
35. Merkel of films
38. Near-prime seating
39. Chocolate bean
41. "The Boy Who Cried Wolf" fable writer
45. Competed in a British bee?
46. Eniwetok blast, briefly
47. Mr. ___ of "Pride and Prejudice"
48. Butter trees

DOWN
1. 700, in ancient Rome
2. She, in Ipanema
3. Indy circuit
4. Capt. Wentworth of "Persuasion"
5. George of "Star Trek"
6. Like some cakes and hair
7. Agcy. spawned by the Manhattan Project
8. Line above the equator: Abbr.
9. Mr. Oleson of "Little House..."
10. Once around the sun
16. It encloses a ltr.
18. Title protagonist Woodhouse
19. A low tide
20. E. ___ (bacteria)
21. Heroine of "Pride and Prejudice"
24. Exam for aspiring drs.
25. ___ extra cost (free)
26. Dionne Warwick hit "I ___ Little Prayer"
28. Orange-colored

31. Chinese philosopher ___-tzu
34. Skater Michelle's family
35. La Jolla campus, for short
36. California wine county
37. Dell or HP rival

40. Liq. ingredient
42. Call, as in cards
43. Female bear, in Madrid
44. A TD is worth six

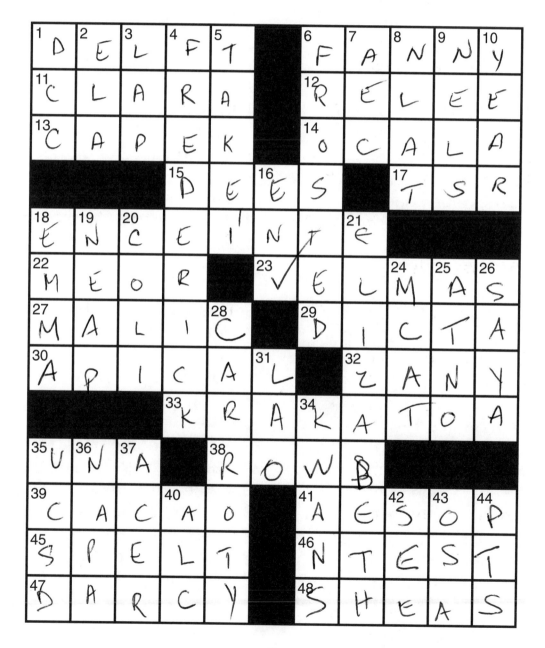

¹D	²E	³L	⁴F	⁵T	■	⁶F	⁷A	⁸N	⁹N	¹⁰Y

(crossword grid, partially filled by hand)

Row 1: ¹D ²E ³L ⁴F ⁵T ■ ⁶F ⁷A ⁸N ⁹N ¹⁰Y
Row 2: ¹¹C L A R A ■ ¹²R E L E E
Row 3: ¹³C A P E K ■ ¹⁴O C A L A
Row 4: ■ ■ ■ ¹⁵D E ¹⁶E S ■ ¹⁷T S R
Row 5: ¹⁸E ¹⁹N ²⁰C E I N T ²¹E ■ ■
Row 6: ²²M E O R ■ ²³✓ E L ²⁴M ²⁵A ²⁶S
Row 7: ²⁷M A L I ²⁸C ■ ²⁹D I C T A
Row 8: ³⁰A P I C A ³¹L ■ ³²Z A N Y
Row 9: ■ ■ ³³K R A ³⁴K A T O A
Row 10: ³⁵U ³⁶N ³⁷A ■ ³⁸R O W B ■ ■
Row 11: ³⁹C A C ⁴⁰A O ■ ⁴¹A E ⁴²S ⁴³O ⁴⁴P
Row 12: ⁴⁵S P E L T ■ ⁴⁶N T E S T
Row 13: ⁴⁷D A R C Y ■ ⁴⁸S H E A S

Answers on page 178.

EDGAR ALLAN POE

ACROSS

1. Dandy sorts
5. Poe's "tintinnabulation" poem, with "The"
10. Sade hit "___ Crime"
12. Roman sanctuaries
13. Poe's horror tale of a man haunted by his deed
15. Above, in poems
16. Bridle mouthpiece
17. Beatles label, once
18. ___, Straus and Giroux (publisher)
20. Get wind of
21. Connery and Penn
22. "To be," for Caesar
23. Not afraid to speak up
25. Quien ___? (who knows?)
28. Winnebago owners, for short
31. Chinese sleuth
32. Lasting a long, long time
34. Pumpkin-carving mo.
35. Architect Ieoh Ming ___
36. School support grp.
37. Poe's "The Pit and ___"
40. Work together
41. Khan in "The Jungle Book"
42. Poe's "The Fall of the ___ of Usher"
43. Fine and dandy, e.g.: Abbr.

DOWN

1. In a ___ pique
2. Vegas casino with the mascot Lucky the Leprechaun
3. Coyote State's capital
4. Religious deg.
5. E. coli, for one: Abbr.
6. Name of several UK rivers
7. Schools, in France
8. Andean pack animals
9. Biting parody
11. Pro wrestling's Captain Lou
14. Meshy door part that ventilates
19. Poe's "Nevermore" bird
20. Title woman of Poe's "To ___"
24. Keeps away from
25. Word with pine or tape
26. "Bless you!" trigger
27. Flat-bottomed river craft
29. "Believe It or Not" name
30. Galileo discovered its rings
33. Adds a handle to
35. Baseball legend Rose
38. Alternatives to Macs
39. Nervous speaker's sounds

Answers on page 178.

BAKER STREET REVISITED

ACROSS
1. Chunk, as of concrete
5. Melodic motif
10. Word before Kitchen or Angels
12. Faced courageously
13. Of feathered friends
14. Not at all well
15. 1988 British comedy with Michael Caine as Sherlock
17. One way to be missed
18. At the stern
21. Brit's 26th letter
22. Done with
26. "The Woman," to Holmes
28. "West Side Story" girlfriend
29. Talkative bird
30. "Life of Pi" director Lee
32. Superb serve
33. Fable messages
36. 1979 "memoir" about adventures of Sherlock's brother, Mycroft Holmes
42. Major arteries
43. Airline seat choice
44. Agreement between nations
45. Blends or combines
46. Drawn-out battle
47. Place for a chin on a violin

DOWN
1. "Pygmalion" author
2. Big name in jeans
3. Got down from a horse
4. Down feeling, with "the"
5. Courtroom drama, e.g.
6. ___ days (happy time in the past)
7. Devil's specialty
8. Bill of fare
9. Jigsaw puzzle solver's starting point, often
11. Clock-radio button
12. With ___ breath (expectantly)
16. "If I Was" singer Midge
18. Align the crosshairs
19. Fish banquet
20. Gymnast's perfect score
23. By way of
24. List-ending abbr.
25. "Boy Problems" singer Carly ___ Jepsen
27. It may say "Hello"
28. Lustrous, poetically
30. Pretentious, as a film
31. "I'll have to pass"
34. Deliver a speech

35. More crafty
36. Diner sign
37. Edible seaweed used for sushi
38. Ancestry diagram
39. Getaway spot in the sea
40. Cutlass or 88, in the auto world
41. Chicks' hangout?

Answers on page 178.

UNUSUAL AMERICA

ACROSS

1. Cheers! and Salud!
7. Noisy clamors
11. Aim toward
12. On the briny
13. Wacky museum in Lawrence, KS, has 350-plus sock monkeys, an Elvis toenail, and more
15. Flash of light
16. Antelope, to a cheetah
18. Williams and Turner
21. Lode finds
22. Inverted v's
24. Quipster or punster
25. Baseball hat
26. Grazers' meadow
27. Like a body temperature of 98.6
29. Throat-clearing sound
30. With 31-Across, one way to see offbeat stuff like 13- and 34-Across
31. See 30-Across
32. Clockwork, mostly
34. 20-foot tall peanut monument in Ashburn, GA
40. Cause for aspirin
41. In the on-deck circle
42. Stock exchange membership
43. Words of assent

DOWN

1. Beret cousin
2. Big Columbus sch.
3. Coll.-level high school courses
4. Lengthy assaults
5. Lionel Richie's first solo #1 hit
6. Large truck, briefly
7. More nutty
8. "Looking for," in personal ads
9. "Air Music" composer Rorem
10. In a blue mood
14. Available, as beer
16. Earlier conviction, in cop-speak
17. In-again fashion
19. New ___ (India's capital)
20. Brew, as tea
21. Confess, with "up"
22. Iron Man Ripken
23. "Casablanca" pianist
25. Naval officer-to-be
28. Refrigerator adornment
29. Firebugs commit them

31. Metaphor or irony, e.g.
33. "___ walks into a bar..."
34. Neon or helium
35. Driving hazard

36. "Mystery solved!"
37. Wanna-___ (imitators)
38. Computer file suffix
39. Some NFL blockers

1	2	3	4	5	6		7	8	9	10
11							12			
13						14				
			15							
	16	17				18		19	20	
21					22					23
24				25				26		
27			28				29			
	30					31				
			32		33					
34	35	36						37	38	39
40					41					
42					43					

Answers on page 178.

SUMMER CAMP

ACROSS

1. Outdoor jaunts at some camps
6. Some South Africans
11. Opted for
12. Figure skater Slutskaya
13. That one/this one/both
14. Sprites of Persian mythology
15. Aspirin tablet
17. First lady
18. "Enough is enough!"
22. "Buona ___" (Italian "Good evening")
23. Tasty treats at summer camp
27. "Kiss of the Spider Woman" star
29. Miss ___ of "Dallas"
30. Summer campers may see a lot of this
32. Overdue
33. Reacted in horror, say
35. "To Kill a Mockingbird" character
38. Hart's mate
39. Get on a soapbox
41. "The prettiest girl ___ saw…" (Start of "Sippin' Cider" camp song)
45. Allude (to)
46. Gemini rocket
47. Like a busybody
48. Vessel seen on many a camp lake

DOWN

1. Initials of fairy-tale author
2. Him, in Heidelberg
3. Decked in a boxing ring
4. Gullet
5. Opera ___ (opera buffa's counterpart)
6. Fun ride at some summer camps
7. British rocker Midge ___
8. Bygone Italian coins
9. Cambridge or Oxford, briefly
10. Self-addressed stamped env., for short
16. Mormon Church letters
18. Book identification no.
19. Aloe ___
20. The "E" in QED
21. NASCAR locale featured in a 2006 film
24. Chowder fish
25. High flier at some camps
26. Bird feeder tidbit

28. Outdoor activity at many a summer camp
31. Verdi aria "___ tu"
34. Ancestor of today's computers
35. Brought into the world
36. "Milk's Favorite Cookie"
37. Clumsy ones
40. Golf peg
42. Title akin to Rev.
43. "Microsoft sound" composer Brian ___
44. "Mittens" singer Carly ___ Jepsen

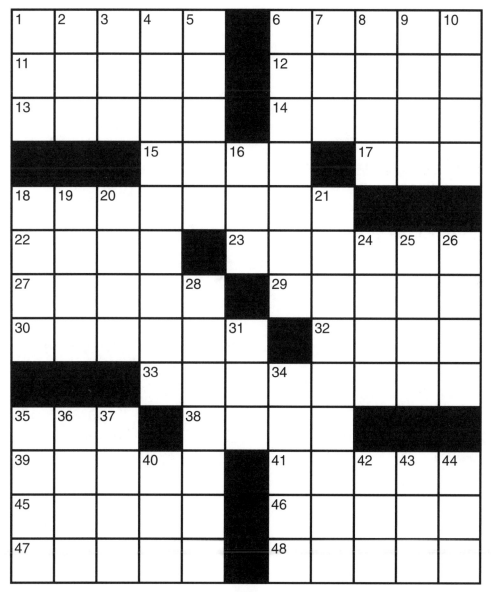

Answers on page 179.

ACROSS

1. Everglades wader
6. Precipice
11. By oneself
12. Helpful sort
13. Highest, on a diploma
14. Carved pillar
15. ___ Building (NYC landmark)
17. Where Innsbruck is capital
18. Not filleted, as a fish
21. Like the acid in vinegar
25. Cicero's "Where?"
26. One way to get directions
27. Coin of old France
28. Jubilant shout
30. Get together (with)
31. Orderly lineup
33. Chicago landmark renamed in 2009
39. Inner self, to Jung
40. La Scala production
41. Piano string material
42. About a drop
43. Store-window posting
44. Appeases, as hunger

DOWN

1. Relax, with "up"
2. Dejected
3. Gambol or cavort
4. Hostile feeling
5. Like some wedding watchers
6. Close-fitting robe
7. Like three famous pigs
8. Think-tank nugget
9. Billiard tabletop material
10. Liberated
16. Blackboard items
18. Bull's motto?
19. "Madama Butterfly" sash
20. A small drink
22. Golfer's peg
23. Diamonds, to a jewel thief
24. Use a saw
26. Overhead shots
29. Golf great Arnold
30. Mr. Magoo's problem
32. Basic units of matter
33. Do a laundry chore
34. Enjoying, in slang
35. Place or stead
36. "They ___ thataway!"
37. Niagara Falls source
38. Battering devices

Answers on page 179.

SILENT LETTERS

ACROSS

1. Bogus deal
5. Money owed, with a silent B
9. "The Alchemist" novelist Coelho
11. "Rebel Without a Cause" actor Sal
12. Gomez Addams portrayer
13. Lay to rest
14. 1 or 66, briefly
15. Payment proof, with a silent P
17. Hard to catch
19. Grade in the 70s
20. Susan Lucci's Kane
21. Cousteau's realm
22. Euripedes drama
24. Drain, as of energy
26. Actresses Stone and Watson
29. Elongated fish
30. Inhale and exhale, with a silent E
32. Snooty sort
34. Grafton's "___ for Homicide"
35. Buffett's hometown
36. Shocking response at the altar?
38. Author Jaffe and former

gossip columnist Barrett
39. "Along ___ Spider"
40. Be a busy beaver, with a silent G
41. Basil, e.g., with a silent H

DOWN

1. Bowler's next best thing
2. Royal abode, with a silent T
3. Truffaut or Hitchcock
4. 1051, in old Rome
5. Chow down uptown
6. Tempt with a carrot?
7. Electronic pager
8. Austrian pastry
10. How scampi may be served
11. Nursery rhyme trio
16. Tax dodgers
18. Likely patsy
21. Bear with a too-soft bed
23. Like ipecac
24. Sockeye, with a silent L
25. "Break Free" singer Grande
27. Back from vacation, say
28. Brawl souvenir
29. Ohm or Solti
30. No-no for judges and journalists
31. Abbr. on a cornerstone
33. Begin to melt
37. Code dash

Answers on page 179.

POTTERY

ACROSS

1. Computer debut of 1981
6. Blue and white pottery of Holland
11. Caramel-coconut Girl Scout cookie
12. Decorative Japanese porcelain
13. "___ is human...": Pope
14. Cane or beet output
15. Certain journalist: Abbr.
17. Abbr. in many French street names
18. Husband of Helen of Troy
22. Blue dye source
23. Rise in the Dow
27. Badge with a photo on it, for short
29. "My Cousin Vinny" Oscar winner Marisa
30. More snoopy
32. Countrywide: Abbr.
33. Eric the Red, for one
35. Under warranty: Abbr.
38. Chess result, sometimes
39. Swahili word for "freedom"
41. "West Side Story" opponents
45. Goldfinger's first name
46. Directive
47. Earthenware pot or jar
48. Asian alliance from 1954 to 1977

DOWN

1. Adherent: Suffix
2. Novelist Bette ___ Lord
3. Defarge or Tussaud
4. Fine china
5. Sing in the snow, perhaps
6. Cause a disturbance
7. Aussie bird that can't fly
8. Doesn't keep pace
9. Keg-party locale
10. Firestone product
16. Indian author Santha Rama ___
18. Popular street name
19. Opposite of "ecto"
20. Faultfinders pick them
21. Ceramic crockery
24. Islamic holy man
25. Former Fed. job-training program
26. Pottery furnace
28. Large clam of the Northwest
31. Elementary education, familiarly
34. Tropical palms
35. Nacho dip, for short

36. Calendar abbr.
37. Spanish silver dollar
40. Ocasek, formerly of The Cars
42. Document that a company may ask you to sign to protect its secrets: Abbr.
43. Comprehend fully
44. "No seats left" Broadway sign

1	2	3	4	5		6	7	8	9	10
11						12				
13						14				
			15		16			17		
18	19	20					21			
22					23			24	25	26
27				28		29				
30					31		32			
			33			34				
35	36	37		38						
39			40			41		42	43	44
45						46				
47						48				

Answers on page 179.

PALINDROMES

ACROSS

1. Carpenter's tool, palindromically
6. Hyphen kin
12. "I Still See ___" ("Paint Your Wagon" tune)
13. Macho
14. Type of cabbage or a London hotel
15. Captivate
16. "Watch out for Fido and tabby!", palindromically
18. Like a runway model
19. "___ make a lovely corpse": Dickens
22. Arch or brew add-on
23. Genetic messengers
27. Middle: Comb. form
29. Traffic cone
30. Actress Remini of "The King of Queens"
31. "Mean Girls" actress Gasteyer, palindromically
33. 90-degree pipe joint
34. Revolted or rebelled
37. One North Pole notable visits Final Frontier org., palindromically
43. Country's boundary
44. Computer that weighed 30 tons
45. Smartphone feature
46. Utah mountain range
47. Problem for wooden ships
48. Chopper topper, palindromically

DOWN

1. "___ is more" (architectural principle)
2. Israeli resort city
3. Exhortation for le roi
4. Stock plans providing worker ownership: Abbr.
5. Time between flights
6. How to divide things to be fair
7. North Dakota's "Magic City"
8. Window treatments
9. Je t'___: I love you, in France
10. Vegas machine, for short
11. Belonging to that lady
17. Biblical father of Abner
19. Stomach acid, chemically
20. Like very wide shoes
21. Forensic material
24. N.Y. Mets' div.
25. "You've got mail" company
26. Tina Fey was its first female head writer, briefly

28. Oklahoma City's NBA team
29. Rabies vaccine developer Louis ___
31. Biblical landfall location
32. Destroyer that picked up an astronaut
35. Prefix meaning "wing" or "feather"

36. Morricone of film scores
37. Alphabet openers
38. Fly high, as an eagle
39. Its mascot is a mule
40. Isn't for some people?
41. Japanese P.M. who won the 1974 Peace Prize
42. Budget Rent-___

Answers on page 179.

HEIST MOVIES

ACROSS

1. 1995 De Niro/Pacino heist movie
5. Brought up, as a child
11. 11th century Spanish hero
13. Hindu drink of immortality
14. "Sweetheart" of "Jersey Shore"
15. Inuit in a 1922 film classic
16. 2008 Jason Statham heist movie
18. "Others" in a Latin phrase
19. Canadian satirist Mort
22. "The ___ Job," 2003 Mark Wahlberg heist movie
25. Culpa preceder
26. Cow's first stomach
27. Convocation of witches
29. Aladdin's monkey pal
30. 1964 Melina Mercouri heist movie
32. Backtalk
34. "That's not ___!" (parent's warning)
35. 1999 Connery/Zeta-Jones heist movie
40. Samantha's mother on "Bewitched"
42. Grammy-winning country star Steve
43. Women's ___ (feminist)
44. Fencing foils
45. Arctic waters, on historical maps
46. Galahad and Lancelot, e.g.

DOWN

1. Command, of yore
2. David and Goliath's battlefield
3. Highest point
4. Pastry shell filled with meat, fish, etc.
5. First elected Congresswoman Jeannette
6. Key of Billy Joel's "Uptown Girl": Abbr.
7. Works by New Yorker cartoonist Peter
8. City in central Ecuador
9. DDE's WWII command
10. Deadwood's terr.
12. Call a radio show, say
17. Actress Long or Peeples
20. Big pile
21. Notes between sol and do
22. 401(k) alternatives
23. Big brass horn
24. Getting a charge out of
27. Epic poem

26

28. Celestial diagrams
30. Lead-in to "boom-de-ay"
31. Wireless communication: Abbr.
33. Stuck-up types
36. Maple or cherry

37. "Able was I ___ saw Elba"
38. Atlanta Brave or New York Met, slangily
39. Trueheart of "Dick Tracy"
40. Yale booster
41. Actor Cage, to friends

1	2	3	4			5	6	7	8	9	10
11				12		13					
14						15					
16					17						
			18					19		20	21
22	23	24							25		
26							27	28			
29					30	31					
32			33		34						
		35		36					37	38	39
40	41						42				
43							44				
45								46			

Answers on page 179.

HASHTAG HUMOR

ACROSS

1. Leftover bit of cloth
6. Golf-shoe gripper
11. "Star Trek" character with a Swahili last name
12. "Donnie ___" (1997 Depp/Pacino film)
13. Dutch colonists in South Africa
14. "___ Room": longtime kids' TV show
15. Hashtag for a movie about a prehistoric pig?
17. Hashtag for judges who are members of the bored?
18. Annoyance for a fairytale princess
21. "Didn't know that!"
22. "___ Kleine Nachtmusik" (classic Mozart piece)
25. Clear the chalkboard
27. Yeti and the Loch Ness monster, e.g.
28. Neighbor of 16-Down
29. A in French class
31. Cheer to a matador
32. Gives a hand at a card table
35. Hashtag for a rock star who has a crush on his guitar?
40. How an NBA game cannot end
41. Native American of Oklahoma
42. Is deserving of
43. Aired a second time
44. Gumby's pony
45. City, to Germans

DOWN

1. Predicate's partner: Abbr.
2. China's ___ En-lai
3. Regretful one
4. Lineup, as of troops
5. Section of a literary work
6. "Bad, Bad Leroy Brown" singer Jim ___
7. Eel-like fish
8. Phil in the Hockey Hall of Fame
9. Chromebook maker
10. Peter, eldest of the Monkees
12. Pickling liquid
16. Its cap. is Stockholm
18. Farm enclosure
19. Suffix with ranch or pistol
20. Termite predator
23. It awards the Stanley Cup
24. Point opposite WNW

26. Term of endearment
27. Heavenly streakers
29. "___ Gold" (1997 Peter Fonda film)
30. Abbr. on a returned check
33. "Jaws" island town
34. Beginning

35. Like a wet noodle
36. ___ cat (sandlot game)
37. Olympic swimmer with 12 medals ___ Torres
38. Brit's cry of astonishment
39. First-of-the-month payment

Answers on page 180.

BOTANIC GARDENS

ACROSS

1. Ornamental houseplant
6. Mojave flora
11. Pirate's "Halt!"
12. Grade just short of an A
13. Dame Nellie of opera
14. Angler's spools
15. "Free Willy" whale
17. Antipoverty agcy. created under LBJ
18. 1954 Fellini Oscar winner
22. 11,000-foot Sicilian peak
23. David of "St. Elsewhere"
27. Claude who played Sheriff Lobo
29. Beyond beefy
30. Bluebeard's last wife
32. Administered by mouth
33. Like many a spring garden
35. Suffix for some email attachments
38. Curly-leaf cabbage
39. Sauce served with fish
41. Do penance
45. Lint-collecting bellybutton
46. Firecracker parts
47. Buddhist flower
48. Brainy

DOWN

1. Kinfolk, for short
2. "___ Got a Secret" (old TV game show)
3. "Silent" president Coolidge
4. First such garden in America, 1842
5. Beatles drummer Ringo
6. Medium for good buddies
7. King Kong, for example
8. Geppetto's goldfish
9. Large bulrush in a marsh
10. "This ___ sudden!"
16. Where a truck driver sits
18. Bit of foliage
19. Island off Alaska
20. Cranky state
21. Tree collection found in many botanic gardens
24. Brand of spongy balls
25. Biblical twin of Jacob
26. Make oneself heard in the din
28. Blue Ridge range
31. Chicken-king link
34. Five kings of Norway
35. Beach toy with a handle
36. Fred Flintstone's pet
37. Type of type
40. "Elementary" star Lucy
42. Mama bear, in Mexico
43. Father of Abner

44. Time zone in Florida

Answers on page 180.

ARTS AND CRAFTS

ACROSS

1. Arts-and-crafts staple
5. Crafty stuff that comes from trees
10. Hemingway heroine in "For Whom the Bell Tolls"
12. Dawn goddess
13. "Pong" company
14. Catch, as a fish
15. Pueblo Indian art
17. Gave a discount to
18. Basketball game played by two people
21. Apocryphal book: Abbr.
24. Company with an "inc." name
25. "As seen ___" (ad phrase)
26. Al Green's "___-La-La (Make Me Happy)"
27. Like chocolates in a sampler
31. Six-line verse form
33. It may be worn at Mardi Gras
38. Popular sleep aid
39. Fe, Ag, Au, etc.
40. Gals' guys
41. Lawn locales
42. Less restrained
43. Hanger for some crafts projects

DOWN

1. Nos. on college transcripts
2. "Kiss Me Deadly" rocker Ford
3. ___ Bator (Mongolian capital)
4. Pendant jewelry item
5. Tito known as "The King of Latin Music"
6. Alpine ridge
7. Big name in denture cleaners
8. "Dancing With the Stars" co-host Andrews
9. Pushed the doorbell
11. Become edible, as fruit
12. Born under the sign of the Ram
16. Blood group letters
18. Its grads are lieuts.
19. Classic drama of Japan
20. Like pencil but not pen
22. Sault ___ Marie
23. Home movie format
25. Tribal precepts, by and large
27. No further away
28. British machine guns
29. "Attack," to Rover
30. Hitting the right notes
32. Ancient Roman magistrate

33. Golf stroke that hits the ground.
34. Life-or-death matter: Abbr.
35. Prefix meaning "gas"
36. Naval rank below Capt.
37. "To be," for Caesar

Answers on page 180.

WHODUNITS

ACROSS
1. Crocodile ___
6. Bride's destination
11. Impressive success
12. Apply holy oil to
13. Wilkie Collins mystery considered the first detective novel (1868)
15. Camera named for a goddess
16. Not the gregarious type
17. Capital city on the Han River
18. Homer's doughnut supplier
21. Bad, in Barcelona
24. Beer named for a Dutch river
26. This John Dickson Carr whodunit is the quintessential locked-room mystery
29. Strike out on one's own
30. "___ silly question, get..."
31. Spot on a peacock feather
32. 1983 Mr. T comedy
35. Used a bat
36. Blackjack card
39. A gypsy curse figures in this suspenseful Agatha Christie tale of murder
43. Like Miss Congeniality
44. Marsh wader

45. African grassland
46. Big, messy mix-up

DOWN
1. Head, in Paris
2. Cave phenomenon
3. Pub brews
4. Bighorn male
5. Got to second base, in a way
6. California's San ___
7. Tolkien trilogy, to fans
8. Barcelona uncle
9. "Barbara ___" (Beach Boys classic)
10. 1 or 66, briefly
12. Like physicals, for many
14. Tic-tac-toe winner
17. Picturesque London quarter
18. 24/7 cash dispensers
19. High point
20. Arm bone
21. Lender's offering: Abbr.
22. Call to Jack Sparrow
23. ___ majeste (high treason)
25. Clean, as a deck
27. Cowboy's frontier land
28. Plague insect
33. Brain, spinal cord, etc.
34. "Citizen Kane" actress Moorehead

35. Citizen Kane's Rosebud
36. Taj Majal city
37. Paul Prudhomme, for one
38. Caesar's rebuke to Brutus
39. Ltr. container
40. Nietzsche's "never"
41. 650, to Romans
42. Car key's place: Abbr.

Answers on page 180.

THOREAU

ACROSS

1. Thoreau essay "___ Disobedience"
6. Thoreau's famous pond
12. Japanese cartoon genre
13. Big name in tableware
14. ___-Hawley Act of 1930
15. Highly seasoned stew
16. A key Thoreau theme
18. "Their ___ Hour": Churchill
19. Greek H
22. Calendar unit
23. Lake from which the Niagara River flows
27. Irish wit Oscar
29. Can't live without
30. Fencer's foil
31. Doctor of sci-fi
33. ATM charge
34. Insertion marks
37. "I went to the woods because I wished to live ___": Thoreau
43. Book after Genesis
44. Like a judge, proverbially
45. Easiest to get along with
46. Lag behind
47. States of equilibrium
48. Very small

DOWN

1. Comedienne Peggy
2. "You've Got a Friend ___" ("Toy Story" song)
3. Cello cousin
4. Departing words
5. Leave on the table, as a casino bet
6. Jo Anne of "Laugh-in"
7. Diarist Nin
8. Will beneficiary
9. "My Heart Will Go On" singer
10. The "E" of N.E.A.: Abbr.
11. Archibald of NBA fame
17. Faline's mother, in "Bambi"
19. Bighorn female
20. Bill bonus
21. A certain pintful
24. Arena arbiter
25. Chlor- or fluor- suffix
26. San Francisco-to-Las Vegas dir.
28. Gets off the fence
29. What a lover of kitsch has
31. Takes forcibly (from)
32. Part of HRH
35. Ill treatment
36. Cache
37. Bear lairs

38. Way out
39. "Livin' la Vida ___" (Ricky Martin hit)
40. Abba of Israel
41. Floral necklaces
42. Every 12 mos.

1	2	3	4	5		6	7	8	9	10	11
12						13					
14						15					
16					17						
			18								
19	20	21		22				23	24	25	26
27			28				29				
30					31	32			33		
			34	35				36			
37	38	39							40	41	42
43						44					
45						46					
47						48					

Answers on page 180.

S.T.E.M.

ACROSS

1. Area of expertise
6. Big books
11. Bronco-busters' event
12. Composed a letter
13. The E in S.T.E.M. could be civil or mechanical, or others
15. Suffix with journal or legal
16. River into the English Channel
17. "7 Faces of Doctor ___"
18. Dividing membranes
20. Spot, in law
23. Onstage curtain
27. Bit of chowder
28. The T in S.T.E.M., briefly—it might involve computers
29. Ending with sacro-
31. YouTube feature
32. "Hallelujah" singer Leonard
34. Approves, briefly
37. "Blazing Saddles" director Brooks
38. It's sometimes stubbed
41. The M in S.T.E.M. includes trig and calculus
44. "The Cocktail Party" writer
45. Brief summary
46. Tech entrepreneurs, stereotypically
47. Fresh with words

DOWN

1. At large or no charge
2. Charge holders
3. A razor has a sharp one
4. Aloha gift
5. Receivers of gifts
6. Brief cybermessages
7. 1970 Stanley Cup hero Bobby
8. Work hard
9. Highest volcano in Europe
10. Bell-shaped lily
14. Not loc., in transit listings
18. Cousin of poison ivy
19. Be a part of, as a film
20. Astronomy or physics, say, and the S in S.T.E.M., briefly
21. Down with the flu, say
22. Mai ___ (cocktail)
24. "Curse you, ___ Baron!"
25. Diamonds, to crooks
26. Electrical conductance unit
30. Halley's and Hale-Bopp
31. Some Range Rover models
33. Bottom line in fashion?
34. Black cat, to the superstitious
35. Healthy salad choice
36. Cookbook verb

38. Muscle twitches
39. Edible tubers
40. Cable TV athletic award

42. Brick-carrying tool
43. 4 o'clock refreshment

Answers on page 180.

SEEN AT THE GROCERY

ACROSS

1. Poultry for roasting spotted at grocery
5. Pancake topping from bees spotted at grocery
10. Blue-and-yellow megastore
11. Cole Porter's "___ We Fools?"
12. Long, slender loaf spotted at grocery
14. Litigious sorts
15. Words to a black sheep, in rhyme
17. Dollar in a jar, maybe
20. Colonial flagmaker
21. Herbal infusion tea
23. Clingy sandwich-covering product spotted at grocery
25. ___ d' (headwaiter)
26. Steak sauce brand spotted at grocery
27. Latv. or Lith., once
28. "Thank you," in Swahili
30. Slander counterpart
31. Pasta go-with spotted at grocery
37. Fenway Park team
38. Growth on a tree trunk
39. Typical Las Vegas gambler
40. Beanery sign

DOWN

1. "What's the ___?" ("Who cares?")
2. Kiev is its cap.
3. Ho-hum grade
4. School in Manhattan (but not in NY)
5. Like the Talmud
6. Bruin Bobby and family
7. Formerly known as, in maiden names
8. Spain's Victoria Eugenia, familiarly
9. Abbr. in a financial report
11. Cereal container spotted at grocery
13. Young scout
15. Ball-on-a-rope missiles
16. Light ___ (almost weightless)
17. Fortuneteller's deck
18. Beyond silly
19. Cartoon skunk Le Pew
20. Engine turns
22. Ballet about Princess Odette
24. Turncoat
29. DDE's rival
30. Do some high-tech surgery on

31. MTV show once hosted by Carson Daly
32. LBJ job-growth agency
33. Some 36-Down workers
34. Tony winner Merkel
35. Morris or Garfield
36. 24/7 service ctrs.

Answers on page 181.

SEEN AT PICNICS

ACROSS

1. Lab bottle
6. Give goosebumps to
11. '50s presidential hopeful Stevenson
12. D-day attack time
13. Beverage holder often seen at picnics
15. Ballpark fig.
16. "Othello" villain
17. 451, in old Rome
18. Indian lentil dish
21. Sultanate on Borneo
24. Desperate, as a situation
25. Grill area built in at some picnic spots
27. "The Mod Squad" character ___ Hayes
28. Desdemona's love, in opera
29. 60's antiwar grp.
30. Air Force hotshots
31. Fiber source in cereals
32. High-level U.S. award
35. Bug protector needed at many a picnic
39. "Okie From Muskogee" singer Haggard
40. Clubs for fairways
41. Hot coffee hazard
42. Baseball's Steady Eddie

DOWN

1. Disappear gradually
2. CEO and pres.
3. Came down, as onto a perch
4. "Do You Know the Way to ___ Jose"
5. "Don't Go Breaking My Heart" duettist, 1976
6. Japanese game akin to chess
7. Jimmy of shoes
8. Company founded by Steve Case
9. Deeply regret
10. Bungle the job
14. Colorful tabby that might be seen at a Maryland picnic (it's a state symbol)
17. "Squawk Box" channel
18. Embassy VIP
19. Seed case
20. Jared in "Fight Club"
21. OPEC amounts, briefly
22. Brand of 35-Across, perhaps
23. Big coffee brewers
24. Actresses Sandra and Ruby
26. Item seen at any picnic
30. Curved like a rainbow
31. Boxing round ender
32. Bit in a bucket

33. Capital of Yemen
34. Classic computer game set on a seemingly deserted island

35. Chats with, online
36. IBM's Japanese competitor
37. Hacienda lady
38. Any NFL or MLB player

Answers on page 181.

LITTLE PESTS

ACROSS

1. Farm produce
5. Line spoken only to the audience
10. Artist Matisse
12. Many Renoirs
13. Cautions
15. Mailer-___ (bounce message source)
16. Soap ingredient, once
17. Big name in chips
20. Scottish seaside resort
23. Held in restraint
27. Beach vehicles
29. Rocket stages
30. Physics particle
31. Tarnish, as a reputation
33. Cousin of a python
36. Writer's body of work
40. Siren
43. Strongly pungent
44. Robotics motor
45. Homeowners' documents
46. Depletes, as strength

DOWN

1. Landlocked African nation
2. Hester Prynne's mark
3. Treater's words
4. Notable
5. Little pest in 40-Across
6. Anna of fashion
7. Groupie's fixation
8. Last word of "For He's a Jolly Good Fellow"
9. Being, to Caesar
11. Privy to, as a joke
14. Breach of privacy, perhaps
18. Brain scan, briefly
19. Ties in surgery
20. ___ Mae (Oscar role for Whoopi)
21. Little pest in 27-Across
22. Suffix with "prop" or "meth"
24. Little pest in 13-Across
25. Fair-hiring ltrs.
26. British mil. decoration
28. Cry from a lamb
32. Butterfly catchers
33. Abacus slider
34. Start of many a story
35. It could be a whole lot
37. Wang of fashion
38. Request on an invitation
39. Those, in Mexico
41. Got behind something, maybe
42. Words from the sponsor

Answers on page 181.

DIME STORES

ACROSS

1. Spore-producing plants
6. Airport whose code is ORD
11. All riled up
12. Bochco legal drama
13. Term for inexpensive variety stores
15. Leave as a castaway
16. Ph.D. thesis: Abbr.
17. Danish astronomer Brahe
19. "Honest" President's nickname
22. Brand of breath mints
26. Retail chain whose logo is a key giving off sparks
29. Beluga delicacy
30. Like some dollars on currency exch. boards
31. Guadalajara girlfriend
34. Abbr. before a colon and a name
37. Period to usher in
41. Aptly named former "dime store" in Australia
43. Held a follow-up conference
44. Words before profit or corner
45. Lessens, as discomfort
46. Slow-moving tree hanger

DOWN

1. Flute in a march
2. Andrews of ESPN
3. Shankar of the sitar
4. Desert trial, for short
5. Posturepedic maker
6. Getting on in years
7. Fish often smoked
8. Et ___ ("and others")
9. Butts (into)
10. Barnyard dams
14. Peach relative
18. Old Hebrew measure
19. "Shark Tank" network
20. TV actress Arthur
21. It encloses a ltr.
23. Devoted attention, for short
24. Comfort's partner
25. "The Lead With Jake Tapper" channel
27. One's bride-to-be
28. Aries animal
32. Door sign at a saloon
33. Bad and then some
34. Good-sized plot
35. "Take ___ Train" (Duke Ellington hit)
36. Allen and Burton
38. Architect Saarinen
39. Budget figure

40. Mother of Jabal and Jubal
42. Chess pieces that can jump others: Abbr.

1	2	3	4	5	■	6	7	8	9	10
11					■	12				
13					14					
15						■	16			
■	■	■	17			18		■	■	■
19	20	21	■	■	22			23	24	25
26			27	28						
29						■	■	30		
■	■	■	31			32	33	■	■	■
34	35	36		■	37			38	39	40
41			42							
43					■	44				
45					■	46				

Answers on page 181.

CONDIMENTS

ACROSS

1. Annoying email
5. Ancient Mexicans
10. Antiaircraft fire
11. Scram!
12. It adds a savory flavor to Asian dishes
14. More glistening
15. Coolers, for short
18. Maritime CIA counterpart
19. Filet of ___
21. "Stately pleasure-dome" of verse
26. Garlicky sauce spooned over beef or chicken
28. Insect with eyespots on its wings
29. Lion's pride
30. Neptune's realm
32. Hip hop's ___ Def
33. Any object of intense dislike
38. Pungent herb that adds zing to salads or sushi
42. Ballpark blunders
43. It's said once but heard twice
44. High-stick pool shot
45. "All You ___ Is Love": Beatles

DOWN

1. Bay area airport code
2. Carry on, as a trade
3. Mouse batteries
4. Dept. that works with Sales
5. Handel oratorio with "The"
6. Turkish bigwigs
7. Fats Domino's "It's ___ Love"
8. Suffix for allow or annoy
9. Crystal ball reader
11. Raspberries
13. Band with the hit "Sweet Talkin' Woman"
15. Spore sacs that are almost a computer acronym
16. Salmon type
17. Highly unlikely, as chances
20. Broody rock genre
22. OT book about a census
23. Composer Khachaturian
24. 1962 Bond film set in Jamaica
25. 180-degree turns, slangily
27. Package recipient's cry
31. Doctor's group: Abbr.
33. "Can I cut in?" noise
34. "When Harry Met Sally" writer Ephron
35. Flight board column: Abbr.

36. General ___ chicken (Chinese dish)
37. Gulf known as "Pirate Alley"

39. Cocktail rocks
40. Any boat, affectionately
41. Brick-carrying trough

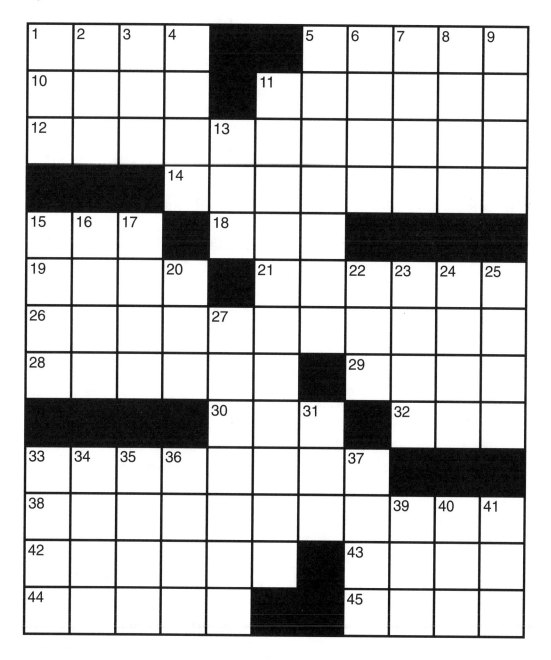

Answers on page 181.

ACROSS

1. Dickens villain in "Oliver Twist"
6. Running in neutral
12. Friend, in Florence
13. Truckers' contest
14. Bathroom-floor installer
15. Classic early press
16. Nickname of Jack Dawkins
18. Riles up
19. Cereal container
22. "Peer Gynt" mother
23. Afternoon event in Chelsea
26. ___ de boeuf: circular windows
28. Sky lights?
30. Actress Saldana
31. Storage units: Abbr.
34. " 'Umble" clerk in "David Copperfield"
35. Fodder stored on a farm
37. Dickens satire of debtors' prisons and British society's attitudes toward money
43. Its capital is Luanda
44. Gabrielle of beach volleyball
45. Dickens' poor-but-honest boy

46. Wegg in Dickens' "Our Mutual Friend"
47. Two-point football score
48. Some carbon compounds

DOWN

1. ___ morgana (mirage)
2. Islamic leader
3. Gold coat
4. Crumbling chunks from a glacier
5. No-hit, ___ game
6. Islamic decrees
7. Dragon of "Kukla, Fran, and Ollie"
8. Hollywood's Cheryl, Diane, and Alan
9. "Got it, man!"
10. Hawaiian goose
11. Active sort
17. JFK alternative in NYC
19. Dickens' pen name
20. Antipoverty agcy. created by LBJ
21. Golf star Michelle
23. ___ kwon do (Korean karate)
24. Before, in old poems
25. Daddy Warbuck's henchman (with "The")
27. Frying pan

29. Word before "lies a tale"
32. Like the eyes just after waking
33. Down, say
35. Franklin heater
36. Spiny moor shrub
37. Land next to Vietnam

38. On Hollywood Blvd., say
39. Weekend-welcoming letters
40. Move, in real estate slang
41. Suffix with canon, class or poet
42. The Durbeyfield girl, in literature

Answers on page 181.

AESOP'S FABLES

ACROSS

1. Humped character in one Aesop fable
6. Bellow from Bossy
9. Chimp or orang
12. Amtrak's "bullet train"
13. Andean edible tuber
14. "Glee" actress Michele
15. Fable about a mouse with a great idea—but who will do it?
18. Bygone dagger
19. "Gross!"
20. Make a choice
23. Fleming and McKellen
25. DNA container
28. Character in four of Aesop's fables
30. Destiny
32. Donald Duck's nephews, e.g.
33. Mix, as cake batter
35. Approval vote
36. Knight's honorific
38. Like "Star Wars"
40. "Might makes right" is this fable's moral
46. Common Market inits., once
47. Reverent feeling
48. Diving duck
49. Character in two of Aesop's fables
50. Minor miscue on the court
51. Bogart's "Maltese Falcon" role

DOWN

1. Calloway who was in "The Blues Brothers"
2. Sleeve card?
3. Blanc of cartoon voices
4. 90-degree pipe bends
5. Kazan of "My Big Fat Greek Wedding"
6. ___ David (six-pointed star)
7. Calendar's 10th, briefly
8. "Hawaii Five-0" setting
9. Medieval quest for gold
10. "Once Upon a Mattress" veggie
11. Chow down
16. Comes closer
17. Coddled items
20. Frequently, in poetry
21. Golf-course standard
22. Divide into three parts
24. Flees (town)
26. Born, on society pages
27. H in Greek
29. Do drudgery
31. Van Gogh flowers

34. Guiding principle
37. Currency of Iran
39. Casino souvenir
40. Earl Grey, for one
41. "Little red" animal in a children's tale

42. Be in hock
43. Org. on a toothpaste box
44. Color of rubies and garnets
45. "I heard him exclaim ___ he drove..."

1	2	3	4	5		6	7	8		9	10	11
12						13				14		
15					16				17			
			18					19				
20	21	22		23			24		25		26	27
28			29				30	31				
32					33	34				35		
		36		37		38			39			
40	41				42					43	44	45
46				47				48				
49				50				51				

Answers on page 182.

ROBERT B. PARKER BOOKS

ACROSS

1. Apt anagram of "notes"
6. Be a braggart
11. Folded Mexican snacks
12. Award named for Poe
13. Spenser and Hawk battle a street gang in the 19th Spenser novel
15. Balcony section
16. Barely squeeze by (with "out")
17. Suffer from overexercise, maybe
20. In literature, Pussycat's friend
22. Life force, in Taoism
23. Like the Cheshire Cat
27. Eighth novel about Parker's Massachusetts cop Jesse Stone
29. Bouncing off the walls
30. Back talk
31. "The Whiffenpoof Song" singer
32. Hair styling substances
33. Charged particle
36. Narrow wood strip
38. Parker's sixth book about his lady private eye Sunny Randall

43. Gold fabrics
44. Boris, to Bullwinkle
45. Vote in
46. Dull photo finish

DOWN

1. Norm, for short
2. "The Way" of Lao Tzu
3. Bygone French coin
4. Barnes's business partner
5. Home to the Kon-Tiki Museum
6. Moistening
7. Admiring poem
8. Dickensian chill
9. Drop the quarterback
10. Yuletide buy
14. More than a swellhead
17. Adolescent woe
18. Fashionable and stylish
19. Like a soprano's voice
21. Lawyer's deg.
23. Most quiet
24. Like a loafer
25. Get just right
26. Hoodwinks
28. Clod buster
32. Accra's nation
33. It is surrounded by water
34. Gem for a Scorpio, perhaps
35. Rumpelstiltskin's secret

37. Opponent of "us"
39. Red VCR button
40. Fish tank accessory

41. Basic time standard: Abbr.
42. CBS symbol

Answers on page 182.

RIDERS IN THE SKY

ACROSS

1. Tractor man John
6. Wide awake
11. Lineup of a sort
12. Muscle-bone connector
13. Celestial archer, usually shown as a centaur
15. Chastises
16. Word with guy or try
17. Get one's ducks in ___
19. Paste partner
20. Relative of khaki
23. Is sore
25. Sign of Aries
26. Alternative to Java or Python
28. Levin and Gershwin
30. Meeting to-do list
34. Pegasus, notably
36. Sherlock's lady friend
37. Gets stuck in mud
38. Coarse grass
39. French school

DOWN

1. Crow cousins
2. Spy novelist Ambler
3. Toy inventor Rubik
4. Sleeve type
5. Optometrist's application
6. Common baseball bat wood
7. Simba or Elsa
8. Make more rewarding
9. Save from danger
10. Messages with hashtags
14. British mil. medal
18. Pentagon simulation
20. Emergency situation
21. Capital of Zimbabwe
22. Pictured mentally
24. Man of the cloth
27. Chow down
29. Croon a tune
31. De ___ (Travis Bickle portrayer)
32. Fencing contest
33. Small African fox
35. Golf-ball prop

Answers on page 182.

PROGRAMMING LANGUAGES

ACROSS

1. Commoner, for short
5. Programming language that sounds all bottled up?
10. Commuter line to Penn Station
11. Old-time bowling alley worker
12. "Did you really think I'd go for that?"
13. "Citizen Kane" actor Everett
14. Programming language that's fun to toss around?
16. Chips sauce
20. Saint called the founder of Scholasticism
23. Scanning ltrs.
24. Programming language that sounds hard to resist?
25. Programming language you'd bend over backwards to use?
27. Botch up
28. Pole carvings
29. Photography pioneer Louis
32. Programming language that sounds just a bit nuts?
36. Hindu holy men
39. Prefix for "space" or "dynamic"
40. Lively and happy
41. Author Janowitz
42. Programming language you might find in a marine mollusk?
43. Programming language that has a lot of zing?

DOWN

1. Programming language that sounds like a positive thing?
2. Describe by drawing
3. Cube designer Rubik
4. Chrome or Firefox
5. Fish organs
6. Name on a WWII bomber
7. Warriors' league, for short
8. Particle that's not neutral
9. Needle aperture
11. Song of Solomon
15. Aloe, for one
17. Capitol crown
18. Long-range weapon, briefly
19. NFL or PGA players, e.g.
20. Achieved a perfect score on
21. Drag-racing org.
22. Marionette maker Tony
25. Greiner of "Shark Tank"

26. Say it one more time
28. Word on all US coins
30. Church guide
31. The same, mathematically
33. Like Pinocchio, later

34. Humorist Bombeck
35. Homebuyer's need, often
36. "What's happenin'?"
37. "Tarzan" extra
38. Alias, to a corp.

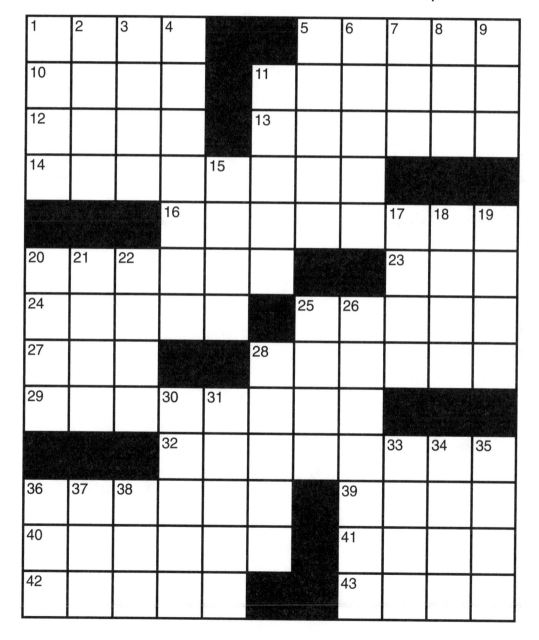

Answers on page 182.

PARADES

ACROSS

1. Apple-pie makers
5. Parade time featuring bonnets and eggs
11. Annual checkup, e.g.
12. Can't stand
13. "Buona ___" (Italian greeting)
14. Lorelei and Circe
15. Auto racing great Mario
17. "As I see it," in email
18. Pre-Mayan people
22. Maternity ward doc
24. Feature of some parades
25. Hide ___ hair
26. Dungeons & Dragons publisher
27. Big name in shavers and coffee makers
30. Sneaky gambits
32. Kind of question with a 50-50 answer
33. Longest wholly-Swiss river
34. Addams' pet lion
38. Fast train in Spain
41. Ankle-length dress
42. Breadwinner
43. Blissful spot in Genesis
44. Parade time in Moscow
45. Kingfisher's home

DOWN

1. Arizona sight or city
2. Animals in a yoke
3. Its Carnival celebrations include parades
4. Flattering, in an oily way
5. Dawn direction
6. Some, but not much
7. Screechy
8. First body part dipped in the water
9. Coastal raptor
10. Feed letters in the blogosphere
16. Astronomical time span
19. Parade of a kind, often for presidents
20. "Piece of cake!"
21. Linemen in front of QBs
22. "Walk ___" (Dionne Warwick hit)
23. Be dull
28. Mean-spirited
29. "I haven't a clue"
30. Bit of butter
31. Non-pro folks
35. British conservative
36. Chops down
37. Auto-glass color
38. Dream-state letters

39. Small battery size
40. Use a crowbar

Answers on page 182.

NEOLOGISMS

ACROSS

1. Color guard's holding
5. Salad-oil bottles
11. Do a stevedore's work
12. Apartment dweller, usually
13. Cyclotron particle
14. Cough medicine ingredient
15. By authority of
16. From way off
17. French military caps
19. Daisy ___ (Li'l Abner's love)
22. Desert rarity
24. Blue-winged ducks
26. Rhyme scheme of the "Rubaiyat"
27. Become unhinged
28. Ragout of roasted game
30. Having bulk and weight
31. Chicago-to-Atlanta dir.
32. Flapjack additive
34. Abbr. in some family businesses
35. Haul with great effort
38. Cajun's craft
41. Relax, with "up"
42. Japanese immigrant's grandchild
43. Richard who played "Jaws" in Bond movies
44. Chisholm Trail group
45. Comes to a finish

DOWN

1. Do a Chicken Dance move
2. Behind schedule
3. Neologism meaning socially inept but charming and cute
4. Emerald or sapphire
5. Neologism for a sci-fi movie about climate change
6. Holiday feast, e.g.
7. Exploitive one
8. "Exit full screen" key
9. Earl Grey or Darjeeling
10. Dry, on a wine label
16. Koko or Kong
18. Big cheese in Holland
19. Neologism for when a guy "explains" something, condescendingly, to a woman
20. Cry said with a sigh
21. See at a distance
22. Backtalk
23. "Witness" actor Lukas
25. Biblical twin who sold his birthright
29. Jerusalem's country
30. Butterworth or Doubtfire
33. Neologism for opposite of a selfie—that is, a conventional photo of someone else

34. Cream of the crop
36. Like hand-me-downs
37. Gooey hair products
38. Science degree

39. Auto club inits.
40. Demolition letters
41. Just manage, with "out"

Answers on page 182.

MYSTERY WRITERS

ACROSS

1. Peach or plum, e.g.
6. Supermodel Campbell
11. Inflexible
12. One who puts you in your place?
13. "The Pelican Brief" author
15. Genteel socials
16. Bk. before Jeremiah
17. Mountain ___ (soft drinks)
20. Soup tin
22. Biological eggs
23. Curving inward
27. His mysteries and thrillers have many a twist
29. Actress Bening or Funicello
30. English "Inc."
31. Edison's monogram
32. Psychiatrist's appt.
33. MPG rating agency
36. Conversational gap
38. TV's "Bones" was based on her forensic thrillers
43. Spiritual mentors
44. Goodbye, in Acapulco
45. What italicized letters do
46. Give a noncommittal answer

DOWN

1. Basketball's Erving, familiarly
2. Copacabana Beach setting
3. "Gross!"
4. Half-___ (pipsqueaks)
5. Barely beat, with "out"
6. Annoyance
7. Biblical jawbone source
8. "I wasn't expecting you!"
9. Ft. or in.
10. Cookbook author Rombauer
14. Storyteller
17. Qatar's capital
18. Novelist ___ Hunter
19. Give a heads-up to
21. Army cpl. or sgt.
23. It makes things happen
24. Having what it takes
25. Ex-servicemen
26. Reaches a conclusion
28. Serve that's replayed
32. Playground ride
33. Cardiology tests, briefly
34. Actor Newman or Muni
35. Gillette razor
37. "The King of Queens" actress Remini
39. Mongol invader
40. "El ___" (Spanish hero)
41. Take all of, as the covers

42. 180 degrees from NNW

Answers on page 183.

LARGE NUMBERS

ACROSS

1. Darns, say
6. Sound heard in jazz and rap
12. Completely crush, as a final
13. Vowel sextet
14. When you need to know what to call a ten followed by 39 zeros, here it is
16. Ballerinas
17. Engages in Halloween mischief, maybe
18. Island near St. Kitts
22. Basic card game
25. Chemist's place
27. Longest Swiss river
28. And if there are 42 zeros, it's this
31. Ford a shallow stream, say
32. Big letters in campgrounds
33. Its grads are lieuts.
34. Horoscope columnist Sydney
36. "All Things Considered" network
38. America's national bird
43. Now we're getting up there—63 zeros!
46. Group of nine
47. Antelope with spiral horns
48. Rudely awakens
49. Measures of force

DOWN

1. Grp. advocating tough liquor laws
2. Its cap. is Quito
3. Gas in some store signs
4. "Say that thou ___ forsake me ..." (Shakepeare)
5. Often, a bell tower
6. Je ne ___ quoi (indefinable quality)
7. Beauty abducted by Paris
8. Engine leakage preventer
9. French for "king"
10. Yours, in Italy
11. "Atlas Shrugged" author Rand
15. "High Fidelity" star John
19. Big name in laptops and notebooks
20. Camaro muscle car
21. Capitol VIPS
22. Common tax form, spelled out
23. Composer Khachaturian
24. Hester Prynne's emblem
26. Eight-gold Olympic swimmer Matt
29. Headgear for Laurel and Hardy

30. Like most jackets
35. Charged toward
37. Pep ___ (morale booster)
39. Ford models of old
40. Composer ___-Carlo Menotti
41. Like Texas's star

42. Concludes
43. Part of KJV: Abbr.
44. Sea goddess who rescued Odysseus
45. Wildebeest's alias

Answers on page 183.

FLIGHT CREW

ACROSS
1. Bird that lays blue eggs
6. "Snowy" wader
11. Keep an ___ the ground
12. "Guys and Dolls" song
13. Acts skittish, as a horse
14. Fake aggie, in marbles
15. Smallest bird
17. Attach with heat, as a patch
18. Knocks the socks off
21. Dr. of rap
24. ___ Coyote (toon with a middle initial)
25. Trapshooting sport
27. It falls away when you rise
28. Like many Oxford buildings
29. Billy
32. Falcon also called American kestrel
37. Lindley of "Three's Company"
38. Of admirals and warships
39. 1930's ___-Hawley Tariff Act
40. Christensen of "Traffic" and "Parenthood"
41. Quarter-back bird?
42. "Nevermore" speaker

DOWN
1. Hebrew R
2. "Hawaii Five-O" locale
3. Glass top
4. List in detail
5. "Forget about it!"
6. Endorse digitally
7. Cajun stew
8. String around a finger, e.g.
9. Arab leader
10. Began a golf game
16. Definite denials
18. Shoemaker's hole maker
19. "Go for the Goal" author Hamm
20. Leader of the pack
22. "Riddle-me-___" ("Guess!")
23. Airport announcement, for short
25. Salmon, at times
26. Ancient Greek instrument that gave us the word "guitar"
28. Jack of "Barney Miller"
30. Swashbuckling Flynn
31. Fireplace log support
32. Enc. with a manuscript
33. Sneaker named after a feline
34. Tel ___, Israel
35. Boat's backwash
36. "Birth of a Nation" group

Answers on page 183.

BLUEGRASS

ACROSS

1. "Bummer!" of old
5. Form assumed by Dracula
8. Not just one or the other
12. Bird of love and peace
13. A, in Argentina
14. Instrument with a double reed
15. Appalachian classic in "Deliverance"
18. Circe or Lorelei
19. Fourteen-line poems
20. Cut into glass
21. One in a highchair
22. First word of many titles
23. Large cask for wine
25. Grass in strips
27. Order at the Pig & Whistle
30. Bad, in Bordeaux
32. Against votes
35. Ship's cargo capacity
37. "Big Three" summit site of 1945
39. Woody Guthrie and Bob Dylan have played this old bluegrass favorite
41. Church image
42. Breakfast staple
43. News spill
44. Forbidden City setting
45. A pocketful, in rhyme
46. Puts a stop to

DOWN

1. Combines to form a sum
2. Danny, on "Taxi"
3. Fend off
4. Choose, as from a menu
5. Burger roll
6. Existential disquiet
7. Forbidden things
8. German capital
9. "___ d'art" (curio)
10. Canine or incisor
11. "Siddhartha" author Hermann
16. Worse than cruel
17. Day, for night
24. One who grouses a lot
26. Possible to accomplish
27. Central, open areas
28. Starlet's asset
29. Poem's farewell
31. Like a Rockette
33. DeGeneres of TV
34. Home or bed ending
36. First of a famous sailing trio
38. Boats like Noah's
40. It never gets lower

Answers on page 183.

BARBERSHOP QUARTET SONGS

ACROSS

1. Convent superior
7. Items on a to-do list
12. Caterpillars and such
13. Puts on the payroll
14. It's practically the national anthem of barbershop songs
16. Getting on in years
17. Muslim prayer leaders
18. Animal trap
19. A little gob
22. Thread weight, for silk, rayon, etc.
25. "___ I" ("Me, too")
26. 1931 tune covered by Sinatra, Dean Martin and many others
29. Does simple arithmetic
30. Pipe sections under a sink
31. Soap ingredient, once
32. Analyze the syntax of
34. "Fiddle-___!"
35. Buddy, briefly
38. Start of a 1931 Hoagy Carmichael song
42. "Great movie!"
43. Faithful wife of Greek legend
44. Persian sprites
45. Bowl or boat

DOWN

1. "And another thing . . ."
2. Cry like a baby
3. Brought up
4. Festive night, often
5. Imitation silk fabric
6. Beacon, e.g.
7. Kind of park or song
8. Feels below par
9. Mr., in Calcutta
10. Barbie's man
11. 180 from NNW
15. ___ es Salaam, Tanzania
18. Confession disclosures
19. Fluffy feathers
20. Adderall target, for short
21. All students at Eton
22. Call on a retro phone
23. Bathtub swirl, e.g.
24. Bump on a log
25. Popeye's ___' Pea
27. Ballet's Rudolf
28. Watch closely
32. Fuels from bogs
33. Ax-like tool
34. 552, in old Rome
35. Certain briefs, briefly
36. Descartes or Lacoste
37. Baseball's Hershiser
38. Abbr. on a pill bottle

39. Baseball's ___ Wee Reese
40. Atmosphere: Prefix
41. ___ in "Idaho"

Answers on page 183.

WEIGHTS & MEASURES

ACROSS
1. Fourteen U.S. pounds
6. Utter unclearly
10. Measure of paper
14. ___ noir (red wine)
15. Make less difficult
16. No longer deceived by
17. Type of alcoholic coffee
18. Yeoman's yeses
19. At the highest point of
20. Farthest down
22. Enjoy a fine restaurant
23. Underwater hazard
24. Added seasonings to
26. The vain put them on
30. The facts, for short
32. Considers carefully, as advice
33. Pasture sound
35. Guest's crash pad
37. 660 feet in horse racing
39. Gets cracking
44. Cow-horned goddess
46. Extreme fear
47. Novel features
51. First car to offer seat belts
53. Fabled Himalayan creature
54. Forty-two U.S. gallons
56. Lay ___ thick (flatter)
58. Nepal's continent
59. Put in the spotlight

65. One sixty-billionth of a min.
66. Robin's Marian, for one
67. Birthplace of Columbus
68. Drop shot, in tennis
69. Former Hawks arena
70. Cerberus guards its entrance
71. West Side Story gang
72. Starch from a palm
73. Clandestine meet-up

DOWN
1. Damage control tactic
2. Lose pep
3. "Step ___!" ("Hurry up!")
4. Small snack
5. Upper regions of space
6. Salts
7. Workforce reductions
8. Puts into service
9. Times to relax
10. Band follower
11. Tempt
12. Made up for
13. Bermuda bikes
21. Occupies the throne
25. Part of a moon cycle
26. Wise-cracking sitcom alien
27. Promissory note
28. President before GHWB
29. The "S" in "RSVP"
31. "Wow!"

34. Unpleasant sound
36. Comprehend
38. Kind of rummy
40. Hear, as a case
41. Before, in sonnets
42. "You Are ___ Alone"
43. ___ Lanka (island nation)
45. On the move on the briny
47. Popular sandwich for kids
48. TV collie

49. Position properly
50. Signs of wildlife
52. Recording room
55. Prom night rentals
57. Dracula's shift
60. Tibetan priest
61. Warm, in a guessing game
62. Garcia of "Ocean's Eleven"
63. Tot's "little piggies"
64. Jet stream direction

Answers on page 183.

U.S. CITIES

ACROSS

1. Book of maps
6. Author ___ Stanley Gardner
10. Madlikova of tennis
14. Ticked and then some
15. Get together with
16. Dedicated poems
17. The Crescent City
19. Arrow notch
20. Volunteer St.
21. The Emerald Isle, to poets
22. Sweetly, in music
23. Color named for a bird
26. Lear's treacherous daughter
29. "The Jungle Book" star
30. U.S. 1, e.g.
31. What rings lack
33. Patron of surgeons
37. Perched on or toy?
39. As reported
41. Sport ___ (off-road vehicles)
42. "The Athens of America" city
45. Small valley
48. Likely (to)
49. Old marriage vow word
51. Home of Graceland
53. Home of the Liberty Bell
57. Poe's "nevermore" speaker
58. Upholstered couch
59. Bring down the quarterback
63. Levine of "The Voice"
64. Ambition
66. Say no to
67. Look at
68. Blakley of "Nashville"
69. Bubbly wine
70. "In ___" (basically)
71. Like oil directly from a well

DOWN

1. "If it ___ broke..."
2. Squirrel's refuge
3. Homeowner's grassy area
4. "Stat!"
5. Sunday delivery, for short
6. Green gemstones
7. Show, as an old sitcom
8. Bruce and Kravitz
9. UFO riders
10. Hawaii's capital
11. "Be ___": "Help me out"
12. Candy wafer brand
13. Slightly off-center
18. Soviet leader
22. Item in the red
24. "Where the Wild Things ___"
25. ___ in "Yankee"
26. Take rudely
27. Sgt. Snorkel's dog

28. Avant-garde sorts
32. "___ the Science Kid"
34. Sundance Film Festival state
35. De Gaulle trademark
36. Inexact figures, briefly
38. Ancient dynasty founder
40. Place for outdoor storytelling
43. Scottish resort town
44. Neighbor of Homer
46. Composer Franz
47. British record label until 2012

50. Agreeable responses
52. Minister
53. "The Devil Wears ___"
54. Underworld of Greek myth
55. "___ to be alone" (words attributed to Greta Garbo)
56. Bounds along easily
60. Hokkaido native
61. Campus lass
62. Leg hinge
64. Barbary primate
65. Rainbow curve

Answers on page 184.

THE BODY HUMAN

ACROSS

1. "Lady" of pop
5. "I love you," in Rome
10. Daiquiri base
13. Space pioneer Shepard
14. "___ there!": tough it out
15. Unreturned serve
16. Draw or paint
17. TV pal of Jerry and George
18. Web address element
19. It absorbs nutrients
22. Wind-sheltered
23. Inverse trig function
24. "It's chilly out here!"
26. Washingtons in the wallet
29. Thumbs-up in Houston
30. Use a harvester
32. It protects the windpipe
37. Tennyson poem, e.g.
39. Simile connector
40. Dickensian "Fiddlesticks!"
41. Decorative inlaid work
43. McGraw of country
45. Orson Welles' "Citizen"
46. Unclutter
49. Monogram for poet Eliot
50. Under-the-sink item
52. Uses a straw, perhaps
54. Fodder container
55. Immune system virus-fight-ers

57. Mention as an afterthought
58. Substance that covers teeth
60. Isn't well
62. Cosmo, for example
63. Signify
64. Corp. money mgrs.
65. Poetic "previously"
66. Red giant in the night sky
67. Brain scans, for short

DOWN

1. "Wonder Woman"'s Gadot
2. Boxers Muhammad and Laila
3. They gave the Hulk his powers
4. Year's record
5. Anklebones
6. "Back ___ hour" (shop sign)
7. Antacid target
8. Diamond or quartz
9. Modest ice cream order
10. Wheel spokes, geometrically
11. Huskies of the Big East
12. Hand (out)
14. Helen in France
20. Lion constellation
21. Tongue-clucking sounds
24. Part of a fedora
25. Make over, as a kitchen
27. Rater of MPG
28. Gretel, to Hansel

31. Smoothed, as timber
33. Football yardage
34. C'est la vie!
35. McKellen and Fleming
36. Popeye's ___ 'Pea
38. Reluctant risers
42. Teeth that tear food
44. Soft tissue found in animals
47. Apartment dweller
48. "Bye bye Miss American ___"
50. Fragrant wood
51. Rocky projection
53. Come in second
54. Starlet's goal
55. Having four parts: Prefix
56. Trudge through sludge
59. New Zealand bird, once
61 Serpent's warning

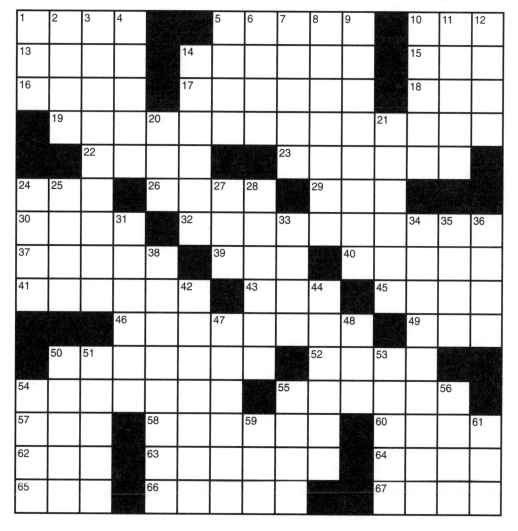

Answers on page 184.

ACROSS

1. Some Hyatt employees
6. Captain Kidd's haul
10. Wife of Charlie Chaplin
14. "Farewell, mon ami"
15. Seniors org.
16. Flim-___ (scam)
17. What kings do all day
18. John Krasinski sitcom
20. Govt. funds for the disabled
21. Rod's fishing partner
23. Clues for trackers
24. "The ___ Report"
    (1976 bestseller)
25. They may be prepositional
27. Pompeo medical drama
31. Eggnog topper
32. Addition totals
33. Stat for a QB
36. "I'll be ___ of a gun"
39. The euro replaced it in Italy
40. Gymnast's perfect score
41. Lake near Buffalo
42. Total square, in dated slang
44. Fountain order
46. "Yikes!"
49. Spanish ones
50. "Funny Face" director
51. Church calendar
52. Show based on tabloid site
55. Long-running BBC program
58. Nevada resort lake
60. "La Bamba" star Morales
61. Farm produce
62. Word used with couture
63. Take a siesta
64. Wimbledon legend Arthur
65. Wise ones

DOWN

1. Roman war god
2. Summer thirst quenchers
3. Old sundial numeral
4. MBA or MD, e.g.
5. It may brighten your morning
6. Shiny cotton fabric
7. Ken of TV's "Wiseguy"
8. "___ You Lonesome
    Tonight?" (Elvis tune)
9. Fed. documents producer
10. Not one's best time
11. Mixtures or medleys
12. Pearly shell layer
13. Make ___ of (botch)
19. Paperwork to fill out
22. Knickknack cabinets
24. Sacred song
25. Seed spitting noise
26. Claire Danes spy series
27. Tiny pest

28. Trojan horse, e.g.
29. Prince Harry's college
30. Lou Grant portrayer Ed
33. Digital recording device
34. Historic plantiff Scott
35. Yemen's capital
38. Like Bill Gates
39. What to eat to lose weight
41. ___ Lodge (budget motel)
43. Uses a sander on
44. "Understood!"

45. Where France is
46. More unusual
47. Yellowstone grazer
48. Old Peruvians
51. "Here comes trouble!"
52. Henchman
53. Speck of dust
54. Sleep symbols
56. "His Master's Voice" label
57. Targets for QBs
59. U.S. motorists' club

Answers on page 184.

ACROSS

1. Baseball stitching
5. Political TV network
14. Heavyweight sport?
15. Evocative of yesteryear
16. Composer Jerome
17. Toughness
18. Catchphrase of the '80s from a Dire Straits song
20. Blue Jays' city
22. Saintly glows
23. Harness strap
24. Indonesian tourist mecca
25. Province home to Montreal
28. Province at Canada's center
32. Hit ___ note
33. Otter cousin
34. Spoil, as food
35. Bus. card nos.
36. Bowling alleys
37. Peace symbol
38. DiFranco of folk rock
39. Mr. Potato Head parts
40. Freelance samurai
41. Mick Jagger, for one
44. Contemporary dragon
45. King Kong and kin
46. Radar O'Reilly's soft drink
47. Rodent on Canadian coin
50. Spot for free drinks
54. "Soup's on" summoner
57. Actress Skye of "Zodiac"
58. Cost to be dealt in
59. All riled up
60. Dinner crumbs
61. Wine label figure
62. Apple utensil
63. Cozy retreat

DOWN

1. Army drill instructor: Abbr.
2. Cash on the Continent
3. Arab chieftain
4. Double-decker, e.g.
5. Film reviewer
6. Attach, as a shirt button
7. School fund-raising grp.
8. Son of Val and Aleta
9. Polite decline
10. Like many an atrium
11. "Finding ___" (Disney film)
12. Art Deco designer
13. Holders of ltrs. or bills
19. Timbuktu setting
21. At no time (literary)
24. Harmful influences
25. Doha's country
26. "___ hooks" (sign on a crate)
27. Borne by the wind
28. Ore collector

29. Down East college town
30. Ox, sheep or goat
31. "Jack Sprat ___ fat"
33. They lived in Chichen Itza
36. "Go for it!"
37. Canada Day was once known as "___ Day"
40. Barcelona chair designer Ludwig Mies van der ___
42. Marge Simpson voice
43. Graf ___ (German warship)
44. German Astronomer
46. "48 HRS." costar Nick
47. Party time, casually
48. One, in Stuttgart
49. Pier, in architecture
51. Inside diameter
52. Cookout intruders
53. Take a time-out
55. Lingerie buy
56. Pencil holder everyone has

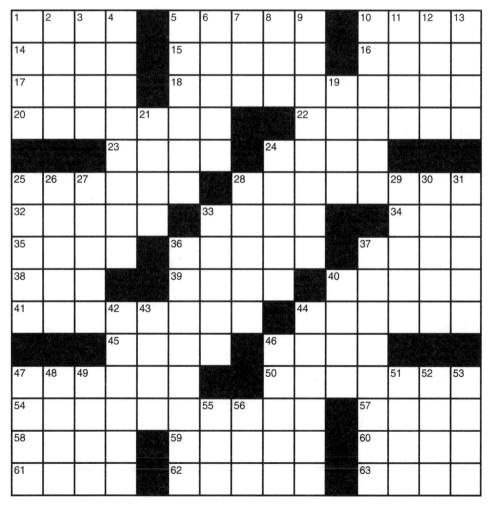

Answers on page 184.

AMERICAN IDOL

ACROSS

1. Bring in, as crops
5. Joint that can be replaced surgically
8. Dirt-and-water mixtures
12. "_____ Enchanted" (Anne Hathaway movie)
13. Be in hock
14. One-named Irish New Ager
15. "American Idol" Season 1 winner Kelly _____
17. Fruity drinks
18. _____ one on (get tipsy)
19. Cause of mental fatigue
21. Hazardous household gas
24. Corn serving
25. Make smooth
26. 2000 Disney musical with music by Elton John
29. Children's card game
32. Use a spade
33. Former "American Idol" judge Paula _____
34. Latish lunchtime
35. "_____ on a Grecian Urn"
36. Ill-tempered
37. _____ down (subdue)
38. Born, in a social register
40. Gas or brake
41. Caterer's food warmer

44. Pull a fast one on
45. Bar mitzvah dance
46. "American Idol" Season 2 winner Ruben _____
51. Fateful day for Caesar
52. Title for Paul McCartney or Mick Jagger
53. Director _____ Kazan
54. Sit for Playboy, say
55. Like the gray mare of song
56. Watermelon throwaway

DOWN

1. _____ room (place to play)
2. Right-angle pipe bend
3. __ carte menu
4. Dolly of Dollywood
5. Vacuum attachment
6. "Letters From _____ Jima"
7. Bic and others
8. Stiller's mate
9. "American Idol" Season 4 winner Carrie _____
10. Hides the gray, say
11. Talk trash to
16. Reunion bunch
20. Blue-green hue
21. Decorate anew
22. Gung-ho
23. Ellen _____, replacement for 33-Across as an "American

Idol" judge
26. "The Simpsons" grandpa
27. Rhoda's TV mom
28. Press for payment
30. Kournikova of tennis
31. Virginia dance
33. Prayer ending
37. Like filet mignon, ideally
39. Wipe clean

40. Pea's place
41. Use FedEx or UPS
42. Heading on a chore list
43. _____ buco (veal dish)
44. Bean _____ (tofu)
47. Up to, in ads
48. Will Smith biopic of 2001
49. _____ Tin Tin
50. NASCAR _____

Answers on page 184.

FAMOUS AMERICANS

ACROSS
1. Tricky billiards shot
6. Will Rogers prop
11. Vietnam War protest grp.
14. Japan's second-largest city
15. "___ Cassio!": Othello
16. Museum stuff
17. African American Chiefs of Staff chairman
19. Law, in France
20. Actress Brittany
21. "Dies ___" (Latin requiem)
22. Comforter fill
23. His biography is titled "One Giant Leap"
27. Clemson's sports org.
28. Smaller than small
29. Stage name of Ehrich Weiss
35. She, in Lisbon
36. Sign-off word, with "Yours"
37. Purpoted baseball inventor
44. Breaks down a sentence
45. Yellow fever mosquito
47. Disappearance of 1937
52. Virtuous one
54. "There oughta be ___!"
55. Double-curved molding
56. Ship's journal
57. "Get Shorty" writer Leonard

59. Racehorse ___ Ridge
60. Before, poetically
61. Civil War side
62. Linguist-activist Chomsky
63. Scoundrel
64. Full of cheeky attitude
65. IRS form IDs

DOWN
1. Comfy slippers, for short
2. "Unto us ___ is given": Isaiah
3. Styling shop
4. Garb for the slopes
5. Suffix with Ecuador or Caesar
6. "Toora ___ . . ." (Irish lullaby)
7. Battle of brands
8. "I call 'em as I ___"
9. ___ Mineo
10. Magic, on scoreboards
11. Pub's cousin
12. Muffles (with "out")
13. Like Scrooge
18. Wrapper worn over a diaper
22. Three, in Berlin
24. More than cold
25. Movie-ad display
26. Like decades
29. Pile, as of rubble
30. Jessica of "Fantastic Four"
31. Worked to the bone
32. Sioux tribesman

33. Neighbor of Braz. and Arg.
34. Name, as a knight
38. Salinger title character
39. Fishermen, at times
40. High-speed Internet letters
41. Renders harmless, as a bull
42. Slow ballet dances
43. Armenia's capital

46. Prepares clams, perhaps
48. Poetic feet
49. Healing plants
50. Before dawn, perhaps
51. Amazes, in a good way
52. Baldwin who was Jack Ryan
53. Wife in "The Thin Man"
58. Meadow

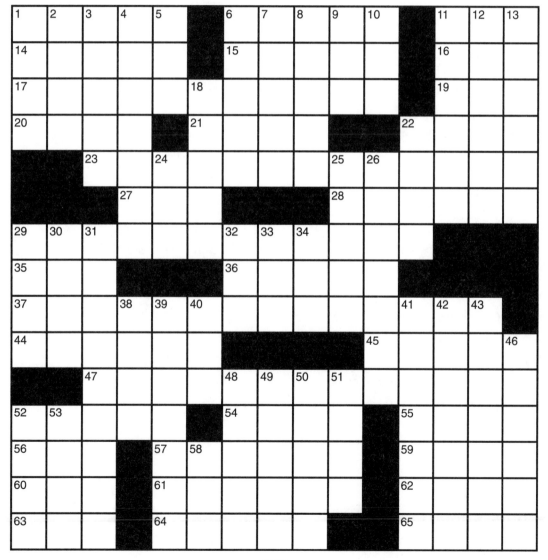

Answers on page 184.

COOKING "P"S

ACROSS
1. Captains' journals
5. Make watertight, in a way
10. Tabula ___ (blank slate)
14. Flitted to a perch
15. Calcutta coin
16. " ___ and the Detectives"
17. Not much more than
18. Pyromaniac's act
19. Tapioca relative
20. Italian cornmeal
22. Tubular pasta
23. Prepare, as potatoes
24. Longtime Indian leader
26. Climbed, as a mountain
29. Puffed muffin
31. Walked in ankle-deep water
32. Dusty and dry
33. Fair lady of Camelot
35. Before this time
36. Sneaky plots
39. Cagey
40. Some hand sanitizers
42. Tears roughly
43. How "great minds think"
45. Becomes more profound
47. Nile waders
48. Stores away
49. Bud supporter
50. Saguaros and such

52. Briefly simmer
56. S-shaped molding
57. The base of alcohol
60. Word ending a threat
61. Mr. Peanut prop
62. New Zealand native
63. Messy barbecue food
64. Liberal ___ degree
65. Seattle hoopster, for short
66. About half of all offspring

DOWN
1. Aladdin's find
2. Toast topper
3. TV show "New ___"
4. Village skyline sight
5. Packed, as in a box
6. Hearing-related
7. Happy times
8. Zodiac's lion
9. Writer Kesey or Follett
10. Put aside
11. Secretary or steno
12. Write on the dotted line
13. Natural skin balm
21. Food and water, for two
22. Vietnamese noodle soup
24. Social standards
25. Rapier with a guarded tip
26. Goodie bag filler
27. Confined, as a canary

28. Teen, e.g.
29. Chick's chirps
30. Poet Rainer Maria ___
32. These get kicked in soccer
34. Tinting agents
37. Work group
38. Single-edge sword
41. Living room benches
44. Loosens (up)
46. Hawaiian party food

47. Slanted, as type
49. "Heidi" author Johanna
50. Cola opener
51. Petri dish medium
53. Dish with some kick
54. Book's ID
55. "The Road ___ Traveled"
57. Printer's dashes
58. Lao-tzu's "way"
59. Relative of sweetie

Answers on page 185.

THE VIEW

ACROSS

1. Sunblock letters
4. Rare golf shot
7. _____-relief
10. Pigskin prop
11. "King of beers" brand, for short
12. Farm female
13. Whoopi _____ of "The View"
15. "Hell _____ no fury ..."
17. The whole ball of wax
18. Reese's "Legally Blonde" role
19. "Laugh-In" regular _____ Johnson
20. V formation fliers
22. Elizabeth _____ of cosmetics
23. Prelude to a deal
24. Daughter of Tom Cruise and Katie Holmes
27. Most AARP members: abbr.
28. Barbara _____ of "The View"
31. Mantra syllables
34. Egg on
35. Prop for Frosty the Snow-man
39. Instrument "on my knee"
41. Former cigarette ad figure Joe _____

42. Twistable cookie
43. Auto takeback
46. _____ soup (thick fog)
47. "The French Connection" subject Eddie _____
48. Rosie _____, formerly of "The View"
50. Tina Turner's ex
51. "_____ the season ..."
52. Poem of tribute
53. Winding curve
54. Porker's pad
55. Take the plunge

DOWN

1. Like hot merchandise
2. Air rifle ammo
3. _____ up (disgusted)
4. Brother of Cain
5. Hair ringlet
6. Upper hand
7. Joy _____ of "The View"
8. Oscars, Emmys, Grammys, etc.
9. Hunter's canine companion, perhaps
13. "Just Dance" singer Lady _____
14. "Akeelah and the _____" (2006 movie)
16. Rare as _____ teeth
21. Do zigzags, say

22. Freebie at some gas stations
24. _____-mo replay
25. Hagen of stage and screen
26. Like a boiled lobster
29. "Many moons _____ ..."
30. Place for a salt scrub
31. Slender woodwind
32. "My Little _____" (Gale Storm sitcom)
33. Moves furtively
36. Slow the progress of
37. Did a KP chore
38. Airline to Ben-Gurion airport
40. Star _____, formerly of "The View"
41. Pull a fast one on
43. Starts to stink, say
44. Trim to fit
45. Flower in a pocketful
49. "This minute!"

Answers on page 185.

BROADWAY MUSICALS BY SONGS

ACROSS

1. Line in a song
6. Egyptian sacred bird
10. "Yuk, yuk" kin
14. British pop singer Lewis
15. Barnes & Noble e-reader
16. Portentous event
17. Hackneyed
18. "Beloved" novelist Morrison
19. "___Language": 1993 read
20. H.S. yearbook buyers
21. "Shall We Dance" musical
24. Illinois' Everytown
25. Deal with a knot
26. Japanese grill
29. Bread of India
31. "People Will Say We're In Love" musical
33. Intelligence, slangily
37. Cordelia's father
38. Navigation aid, for short
40. Mine find
41. Sponge gently
42. Native-born Israeli
45. Adorable one
47. Biblical word on a wall
48. Satirize
50. "Luck Be a Lady" musical
54. Exams for future attys.
55. Early roadsters
56. Encyclopedia Brown job
60. Alley Oop's love
61. "Just Like Paradise" musical
63. Unique person, in old slang
64. "Explorer" of cartoons
65. Bedside buzzer
66. Boot-camp cuisine
67. Tan and Schumer
68. Brief and to the point

DOWN

1. Lawyers' degrees
2. Date on a penny
3. Howard and Jaworski
4. Lightning ___ bottle
5. W. Coast engineering school
6. Temporary period
7. First in a multi-volume set
8. Sea between Greece and Italy
9. It's all around you
10. Hallelujah kin
11. Botanical spike
12. Fictional Alpine miss
13. "Little Girls" musical
22. Chocolate Hostess snack
23. American Pacific territory
24. Jack of classic TV
26. Hammerlock or full nelson
27. Big name in furniture
28. Be a tattler
30. Balaam s beast

32. Farming dept.
34. Former newspaper section
35. Destiny's Child was one
36. Not out of view
39. Inept boxers, in slang
42. Coral and China
43. Jillian or Coulter
44. Boudoir
45. 950, in old Rome
46. Like Rodeo Drive shops
47. Some red dwarfs

49. "And furthermore..."
50. Euphoria's opposite
51. Maine-to-Florida hwy.
52. Some locks
53. Express disapproval of
57. Culture medium
58. Sun. talks
59. Girl in a Salinger story
61. Abbr. on a vitamin bottle
62. Having a spare tire, maybe

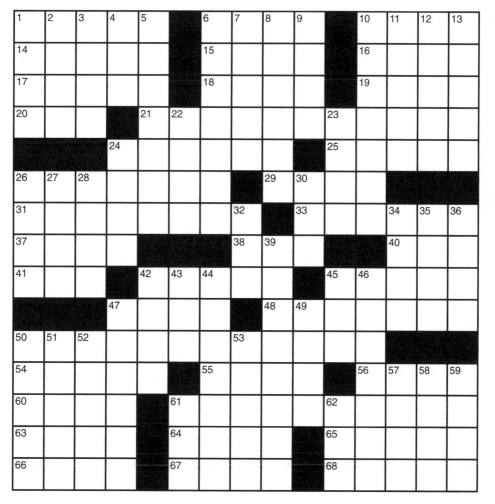

Answers on page 185.

BEST PICTURE OSCAR WINNERS

ACROSS
1. Access onto the highway
5. 4th and long play, often
9. Nothing, south of the border
13. Countess's spouse
14. Crazy way to run
15. Brother of Sneezy
16. 2011 black and white film
18. Florida lizard
19. Not a single person
20. Sports drink suffix, perhaps
21. Sit out the vote
24. 1986 Charlie Sheen war flick
28. Grooms feathers
29. Et ___ (and others): Lat.
30. Brain and spinal cord: Abbr.
31. Alaska or Okla., once
32. Opera highlights
33. Early nuclear org.
34. 1961 gang musical
38. Part of an ID
39. Devil's domain
40. Pale blue hue
42. Ozark ___ of comics
43. Teheran's country
44. Journalist Alexander et al.
46. 2014 Michael Keaton role
48. Electronic illustrations
49. "Son of" in Arabic names
50. Loose-fitting dress

51. Venice "street"
54. 2000 Russel Crow drama
58. "Skyfall" vocalist
59. "The Bachelor" prop
60. Anemic one's need
61. Pointillist's points
62. Gets a glimpse of
63. Calif. wine valley

DOWN
1. Abbr. for a professor emeritus
2. "Feels so good!"
3. Desert Storm chow, briefly
4. Flower boxes
5. Creole, e.g.
6. Golden Gophers' sch.
7. Cyrano's famous feature
8. Box office purchase, for short
9. Nine-piece band
10. Abbr. on mail to a soldier
11. Actor Benicio ___ Toro
12. Sailor's affirmative
15. Arp or Duchamp
17. Brown-and-white horse
20. Word on a wanted poster
21. Well put
22. Cold one, slangily
23. More tranquil
24. Carries on, as a trade
25. Musical "sweet potato"
26. Common lease span

27. Group that advises the pres.
29. Forest in "As You Like It"
32. Quinn of "Elementary"
35. Sewer's protection
36. Wrap brand
37. Whitman poem opener
38. Lisa to Bart or vice versa
41. WWII landing craft
44. Playground favorites
45. Stereo system of yore

47. Uses a rotary phone
48. Run in pursuit of
50. Word with -eyed or gin
51. Bounder
52. Commotion
53. Amount after costs
54. Canine sounds
55. Singer's nonsense syllable
56. Alley ___ (basketball move)
57. Genetic "messenger"

ANIMAL WORDS

ACROSS

1. A male deer, or partnerless
5. Sneezin' reasons
10. Wheat or soybeans
14. State of Columbus
15. Skin-soothing ingredients
16. Type of hoop
17. Fat in the can?
18. Holy book
19. Bird of the Nile
20. Fade-out, in movies
22. Shoe like a clog
23. Fencer's blade
24. Humorous word for "think"
26. Reporters' angles
29. Jeeves's boss, formally
32. Accent over an "n"
33. But, in Berlin
35. Bit of data
36. Eminem's genre
37. Linen fabrics
40. About one billion years
41. "Snake eyes" pair
43. Angler's hope
44. Ill-gotten profit
46. Victoria's Secret purchase
48. You've got problems if one of these is on your back
49. Hoists
50. Girl in a kilt
51. Doesn't go on
53. Reagan's decade
57. To complain, or a fish
58. A spiteful woman, or a fox
60. Wander far and wide
61. Author Sarah ___ Jewett
62. Spin doctor's concern
63. Fills with wonder
64. Dick Tracy's love
65. Sky streaker
66. Quarterback's specialty

DOWN

1. "Gone!" at auctions
2. Peanut-sauce cuisine
3. Makes known, as grievances
4. Unexpected blessing
5. Sends a telegraph to
6. Popeye's Oyl
7. Ear or brain section
8. Its cap. is Dover
9. Chicago-to-Miami dir.
10. Italian table wine
11. Gawk on the highway
12. Little bit of everything mix
13. Time traveler's destination
21. Made a choice
22. Paul McCartney's title
24. Beyond rotund
25. Make coffee, in a way
26. Barber's sharpener

27. Tropical vine
28. Swiss herders' instruments
30. Earlier, archaically
31. Pounds and marks
33. Not quite right
34. Stepping up the the plate, or a nocturnal animal
38. Help with the heist
39. Walk through melting snow
42. Plains of Siberia
45. Remove, as from a car seat

47. No ___, ands or buts
48. Fridge decoration
50. Feudal lord, or his subject
51. Connery, by birth
52. Shipping weight allowance
53. Final or midterm
54. "Field of Dreams" setting
55. Nights before holidays
56. Psychiatrist's appt.
58. London theatre, The Old ___
59. "As I see it," in an email

Answers on page 185.

10-LETTER WORDS

ACROSS
1. Part of a window
5. Russian mountains
9. Health orgs.
13. Repugnantly hateful
16. Quite a lot
17. Like an especially tasty dish
18. Concorde fleet, once
19. "___ say it?"
20. U.S. 1 and U.S. 66
22. African tea leaves
23. Pointer Sisters "___ Excited"
25. Study, with "on"
27. King Arthur's was round
30. At ___ rate (regardless)
32. Have regrets over
33. Magic, on a scoreboard
34. Body that includes SHAPE
36. Cannon loader
39. Italian "ones"
41. The Internet or online world
43. Football legend Knute
45. Mormon Church inits.
46. Where to see Mt. Rushmore
47. Hyundai rival
48. Letters on some party invites
49. ___ keyboard (types)
50. Hope to achieve
52. Classic computer game
54. Thumb, as a ride

55. Easy win
57. Really funny
60. Tennis situation after deuce
62. A sapsucker bird
65. Building lot
66. Setting apart
67. Area in London or New York
68. Clean and tidy
69. Dropped in the mail

DOWN
1. Apartment, slangily
2. Like many of us at midnight
3. The Big Easy, familiarly
4. Food Network's "___ Live"
5. They're against
6. When doubled, a Teletubby
7. Inc. or Ltd.
8. Volunteer's offer
9. ___ "Pinafore" (comic opera)
10. Costume party
11. Like draft beer
12. Kind of analyst: Abbr.
14. Hockey players
15. Wide shoe size
21. Gilbert and Teasdale
24. Like Cheerios, say
26. Sells in a bear market
27. Travel by bus, say
28. Cartoonist Peter
29. Person who forges iron

31. In a high-minded way
35. Power serve, perhaps
36. Amtrak and B&O
37. High Andes plants
38. Metric prefix meaning ten
40. Play sporadically, like a CD
42. Land conquered by David
44. Hair removal brand
48. Sing the blues about
49. Wedding seater
50. TV sound signal
51. T. ___ Price (investment firm)
53. Bother with barks
54. Four-string guitar
56. Look carefully (over)
58. Dust-bowl migrant
59. Al Gore's state, briefly
61. Keanu's role in "The Matrix"
63. Abbr. after Elizabeth Warren's name
64. Col.'s outfit

Answers on page 185.

WORLD HISTORY

ACROSS
1. "No ___, no foul"
5. Enliven
10. Lasses' counterparts
14. Frenzied way to run
15. Baseball Hall of Famer Edd
16. Region
17. Winner of 26 Oscars
19. Newspaper opinion piece
20. Japanese title until 1867
21. Answer to "Is that you?"
23. Overhead trains
24. IV dosage amts.
26. Online chats, for short
27. William I's nickname
33. Skewered Thai dish
36. Father of Oedipus
37. Ending for "ranch"
38. Gently-worn, as clothes
39. Far from talkative
40. Boat backs
41. Comb insect
42. "No ___, Bob!"
43. Cheese or chard
44. Shortest president
47. Degree in religion
48. Transmission type: Abbr.
49. Venomous serpent
52. Stevenson's island
57. Chinese pork dish

59. Sledding slope
60. He took the capital of the Sung Dynasty in 1276
62. "Anything ___?"
63. River near the Vatican
64. Trickster of Norse myth
65. Dashing style
66. Retract a comment
67. "Never Wave at ___"

DOWN
1. Anchor rope hole
2. "___ and the Night Visitors"
3. Hershey caramel candies
4. Dept. that works with Sales
5. "Purple Rain" singer
6. Dawn goddess
7. Small and weak
8. Lawsuit benefactor
9. Mr. America's source of pride
10. Founder of Taoism
11. Some Dada paintings
12. Consider to be
13. "No Ordinary Love" singer
18. Small state ruled by a duke
22. Don of radio fame
25. Eyeball covering
27. Insignificant amount
28. Rowed, as a boat
29. Some Japanese-Americans
30. Get a new mortgage, briefly

31. Food crumbs
32. Colonial flagmaker
33. Predicate's partner: Abbr.
34. Not ashore
35. Be crawling (with)
39. Legendary African outpost
40. Beard on barley
42. Air France retirees of '03
43. "Me too"
45. Big Sur institute
46. Namesake of many churches

49. Put on ___ (entertain)
50. Zulu warrior king
51. Carthage-related
52. Quaker's "you"
53. Little stream
54. Maxwell or Schiaparelli
55. Damage irreparably
56. Dies down
58. The Sooner St.
61. Meadow, in verse

Answers on page 186.

WEIRD NATURE

ACROSS
1. Israeli politician Abba
5. Gully fillers
10. Put ___ on (limit)
14. Uncommon, avis-wise
15. Bert's Muppet buddy
16. French writer Pierre
17. A meteorite from the moon was found on this continent
19. "Spamalot" creator Idle
20. Crack, as a secret message
21. Aliens, for short
23. Bump-log link
24. Homes for genies
25. Artist's portfolio
27. Singer DiFranco
28. Amazon's smart home device
31. They have three eyelids
32. "Largemouth" fish
34. Univ.'s cousin
36. San ___ (Silicon Valley city)
37. Speak in flowery language
40. Gamal ___ Nasser of Egypt
43. Therefore, in a proof
44. Like look-alikes
48. Emulates Rip Van Winkle
50. Abbr. on a cornerstone
52. Gold ingot
53. The great horned owl's

"horns" are made of these
55. Causing goose bumps
57. Syst. for hearing impaired
58. Sky deity
59. Sneezy flower dust
61. Q queue?
63. Ali Baba's magical command
66. Friends, in France
67. A Nevada city
68. "Time ___ a premium"
69. Capitol VIPS
70. Boss's nerve-racking note
71. Europe's largest volcano

DOWN
1. Swing or Victorian, e.g.
2. Cowboy's neckwear
3. Greek goddess of the moon
4. Racial equality gp.
5. Stamp for an incoming pkg.
6. Prado works
7. Ending of some pasta names
8. More affable
9. Hub for Alaska Airlines
10. Popular draft pick
11. Headgear for a prince
12. Like a formerly asleep foot
13. "Guernica" painter
18. Flower for Valentine's Day
22. Hindu sage
24. Chemist's hangout

25. "___ Claiborne" (King novel)
26. Colorful Apple computers
29. 210, to Claudius
30. It "springs eternal"
33. Like candy
35. Crickets "hear" with this body part
38. Dominant, in a wolf pack
39. One of the sandbox set
40. To the extent that
41. Confessional opening
42. Gave a hand to

45. Side by side
46. Guy who's got your back
47. Old "before"
49. Madrid misters
51. Proofreader's mark
54. Madras money
56. Borden mascot
59. ___ Penh, Cambodian city
60. Bone: Prefix
62. Aircraft carrier letters
64. Houston-to-Boston dir.
65. Airport info, informally

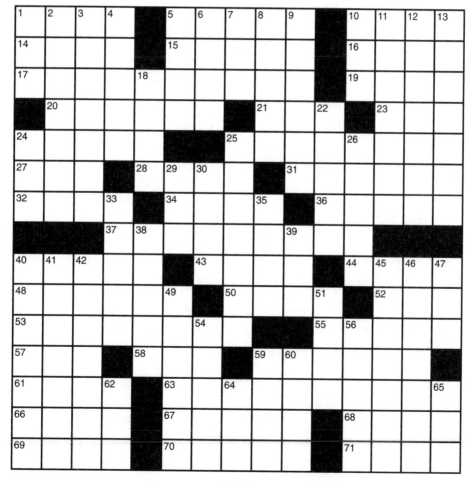

Answers on page 186.

SHAKESPEARE

ACROSS
1. Light bulb gas
6. City built on seven hills
10. New Deal pres.
13. Anklebones
14. Director Kazan
15. All there upstairs
16. Play featuring Ariel
18. City planner's map
19. Angry feeling
20. Average grade
21. Is so inclined
23. Camper's light
25. "___ late than never"
26. Semi-serious "I see"
27. Anagram of "stifle"
30. Bermuda setting: Abbr.
31. Gym pad
33. Pinocchio's goldfish
34. Mil. posts
35. Barely got (with "out")
37. "... against a ___ of trou-
    bles": Hamlet
38. Football officials, briefly
40. "Aladdin" hero
41. Adam Smith's subj.
43. MD's org.
44. Employee ID, often
45. "Stately pleasure-dome"
47. Offshoot denomination

51. Seal engraved on a ring
53. He killed Desdemona
55. Loosens, as sneakers
57. "Simpsons" bartender
58. Call before a "do-over"
    serve
59. Bubbly brand
60. Visibly embarrassed
63. Historic periods
64. Small case for needles
65. Not at all wordy
66. Sun. morning talk
67. Nothing, in Nantes
68. More crafty

DOWN
1. Historic Hun
2. Full of that old school spirit
3. Salad veggies
4. Bone: Prefix
5. Eleanor Roosevelt, to Teddy
6. Admonition to sinners
7. "Bravo!" at a bullfight
8. Catchall category, briefly
9. Fit to consume
10. Shakespeare's fat knight
11. They determine paternity
12. Snappy comebacks
15. Young barracuda
17. Kind of badge for a Scout
22. Mend one's ways

24. Big book
28. La Scala segment
29. Highest note, old style
32. Madison Ave. VIP
35. Setting for most of "Hamlet"
36. Foolish tragic monarch
37. Ben, to Jerry Stiller
39. Freedom from worries
40. Presupposes
42. Party food provider

43. Vehicles
46. GoDaddy purchase
48. Queen of mysteries
49. "Monty Python" comic John
50. Be shaky on one's feet
52. Cole and Turner
54. Microwaves, as leftovers
56. Org. looking for aliens
61. Expected soon
62. Actress Barbara ___ Geddes

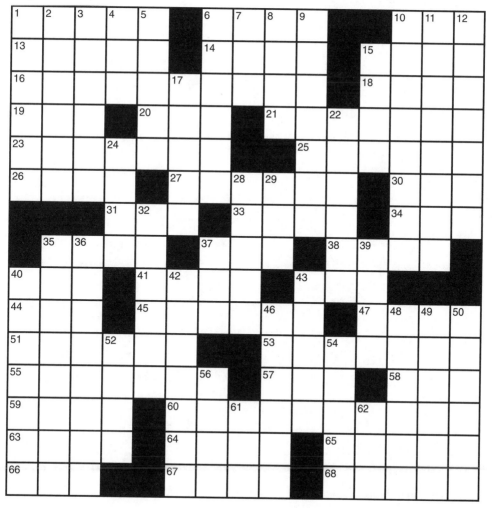

Answers on page 186.

SCIENCE

ACROSS
1. Diner sign
5. Quantity of grain or arrows
10. Takes a chair
14. Actress Sorvino
15. "The Neon Bible" author
16. Opera highlight
17. Any Beatle, once
18. You get a charge out of it
20. Popular online lectures
22. "Siddhartha" novelist
23. Domed home: var.
24. Art colony near Santa Fe
26. Angiosperms and ___
30. Vanna's cohost
33. Equipped, as a rowboat
34. Opposite of messy
35. Regret
36. Electrical resistance units
37. Cotton-candy holders
39. Pet-shop purchase
40. Rock band ___ Fighters
41. Rights group, for short
42. Poet Wystan Hugh
43. ___ Kippur (Jewish holiday)
44. Class of rock
47. Covers with turf
48. Atlanta's arena, once
49. Essential fluid
52. Psychosurgical procedure
56. All politics, to Will Rogers
59. Arch with a double-S shape
60. "Ah, OK"
61. American fur tycoon
62. Mongolia's ___ Bator
63. G-men and the like
64. Whistles of relief
65. Gymnasts' perfect scores

DOWN
1. Give off, as light
2. Aptly named assistant
3. Did not step lightly
4. Chowder go-with
5. Moonshine machines
6. Connect, as a stereo
7. Unfathomable stretches
8. Boxer Muhammad
9. Casablanca headgear
10. Fills and then some
11. Pigmented eye part
12. Padre's brothers
13. Entirely sensible
19. "___ of golden daffodils..."
21. "___ among men"
24. Baobab or acacia
25. Amo, ___, amat
26. Mickey's pal
27. Brute in "Gulliver's Travels"
28. 1983 Michael Keaton family comedy

29. That bored feeling
30. "The Devil Wears ___"
31. Hole-making tool
32. Relative of itty-bitty
37. Incl. on the distribution list
38. Cutlass or 88, informally
39. "Stop that!"
41. Stick out like ___ thumb
42. The A of A.D.
45. Milked animal, to a tot
46. Campfire leftovers

47. Tennis champ Monica
49. Young stray child
50. Altar end of a church
51. Festooned with Charmin
52. Strings for a minstrel
53. Eyeball rudely
54. Like Mr. Mustard
55. Longs (for)
57. Carpenter's cutter
58. Burnt residue

Answers on page 186.

ACROSS

1. Apt rhyme of "aahs"
5. Canadian author Farley
10. Do laps in the pool
14. Bouncy tune
15. Words at a well
16. "Say it isn't so!"
17. Old form of Italian musical
19. Auction offers
20. Attacks from all sides
21. Austen heroine
23. Abbr. on a calendar
24. Seeming eternities
26. More than needed
28. Request a date
30. From Laos or Tibet, e.g.
31. Drain of northern Italy
32. Less constrained
34. Site for moguls
37. Axe handle
39. Caribbean cruise stops
41. Actor Hemsworth
42. "Crocodile Rock" singer John
44. Every book has one
46. Cousins of aves.
47. Prosperous periods
49. Sudden silences
51. Egyptian Sun God
53. Cum laude modifier
54. Moo goo ___ pan
55. Silent clown
57. Fencing ploys
61. Egypt's longest river
63. "Mmm, yum!"
65. Powerful U.S. dept.?
66. Diarist Nin
67. Words before snag or homer
68. Joins in matrimony
69. Alaska, often, on maps
70. Hardly a walk in the park

DOWN

1. Neatnik's nightmare
2. Accessory for Sherlock Holmes
3. Brewpub array
4. Sign of a bad window washer
5. River on Nebraska's flag
6. Have debts
7. Mess behind a computer
8. "As Sure ___ Standin' Here"
9. River at Windsor
10. React to a tearjerker
11. Recording of rain, maybe
12. Longest river in Pakistan
13. Grandma of art
18. Dined on, biblically
22. Center of rotation
25. Blasts from the past, briefly
27. Word with curtain or cattle

28. "Be ___!" ("Help me out!")
29. Egg order
30. "Queen of Soul" Franklin
33. Yale rooter
35. New England team,
    for short
36. Some printing dashes
37. At. no. 2's symbol
38. Goofy or Daffy, e.g.
40. Thrilla in Manila, e.g.
43. "Cheers" regular
45. Anglo-Saxon slaves

48. Tiki bar drink
50. Ashbury crosser
51. Vice President Spiro
52. Bar Harbor's state
53. Badlands plateaus
56. "Buddenbrooks" author
58. Black, at the roulette table
59. Bag for shopping
60. Mount Rushmore's st.
62. Hectic hosp. sections
64. Gift in a long, thin box

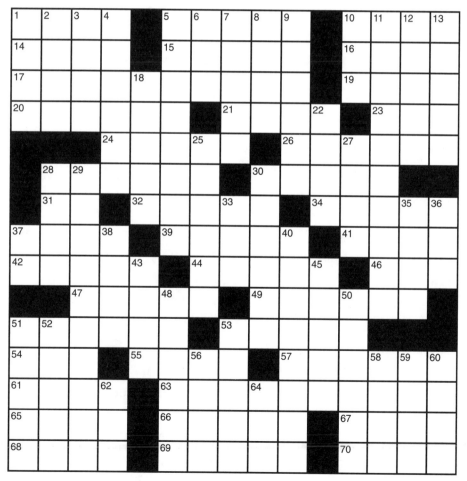

Answers on page 186.

PAINTERS

ACROSS

1. Watery expanses
5. Newborn cow
9. Spanish dim sum, sort of
14. Came down, as onto a perch
15. "Carmen" showstopper
16. Not appropriate
17. Terhune's "___ Dog"
18. Gas used in bright lights
19. High-tech classroom
20. Grant Wood's 1930 painting
23. "Law & Order: ___"
24. Not a soul
25. Hoosier pro hoopster
31. See fit
32. Commanded, old-style
33. Crude resource
36. Painter known for his supper
40. Magazine staffers, for short
41. City of northern Finland
42. Get the better of
43. He developed cubism
46. "Nana" author Zola
48. Dorm monitors, briefly
49. Painter known for dripping
56. Jauntily cheerful
57. Chestnut-colored horse
58. Second word in a fairy tale
59. Poker player's declaration
60. Devoid of duds
61. Half a Hawaiian fish
62. Kitchen add-ons?
63. Backyard storage structure
64. Story framework

DOWN

1. Casa room
2. Actor Jack of old Westerns
3. ___-de-camp
4. Aries or Scorpio, e.g.
5. Yucatan spring break resort
6. Surface measure
7. Cowardly Oz visitor
8. Jack London's "White ___"
9. Walk furtively
10. Common nautical tattoo
11. Michael of "Monty Python"
12. Speedily, to bards
13. Degree in religion
21. A former Mrs. Trump
22. ___ year (annually)
25. Doing nothing
26. "All You ___ Is Love": Beatles
27. God, in Granada
28. "Straight Up" singer Paula
29. Francesca's love
30. Find the sum of
33. Low bills
34. Hosp. areas for the gravely ill

35. Fat-removal surgery, briefly
37. After-bath wraps
38. Not shy with one's opinion
39. Struggling, as a pitcher
43. Deli dill
44. Hydrocarbon groups
45. Did a pressing chore
46. Remove a DVD
47. Edvard Munch painted this

man's death
50. Celestial spheres
51. Bible boatwright
52. Skin, as an apple
53. October's gem
54. Salmon type
55. Create with needles
56. Dessert served in wedges

Answers on page 186.

ACROSS

1. Fox crime series
6. Look over hastily
10. Bridge length
14. Crusoe, before Friday
15. Jimmy of shoes
16. Big name in detergent
17. Yarn-haired redhead
19. Mohammed ___ Pahlavi
20. The "S" in GPS, briefly
21. Term with tuna or patty
22. Anansi of African myth
24. Fishing-rod attachment
25. 1986 book by rocker Turner
26. Former Fuji competitor
29. Marmalade-loving bear
33. Weaving devices
35. Inari is the god of this in Japanese mythology
36. Screwball comedian Philips
37. Actor Gulager
38. Second-rate boxer
41. Civil War soldier, for short
42. On top of, poetically
43. Got ___ rap: falsely accused
44. Roomy size
46. Missing-child bulletin
50. Like Pinocchio, eventually
51. "Would you like to see ___"
52. Party throwing a party
54. Heaven of Norse mythology
56. Color on a windshield
57. Fashion's bottom line?
60. Kings from the East
61. Sunkist product
64. First-year law student
65. "Fiddler" of old Rome
66. Apartment vacancy sign
67. Sun. orations
68. Drains strength from
69. Graceful paddlers

DOWN

1. Happy hour sites
2. Neutrogena rival
3. Rich yuletide quaffs
4. MIT grad, often
5. Dreaded teacher's note
6. Six-headed monster
7. Informal conversation
8. Get an ___ (ace, as a test)
9. Like Teflon-treated pans
10. Cat's-cradle need
11. Apartment for occasional use
12. Axelike tool
13. Just steps away
18. Like one end of a pool
23. Melatonin gland
24. Hit headfirst

25. Prefix meaning "personal"
26. Big name in aluminum
27. Defender of the Jews
28. Homer
30. Suffix with air or hippo
31. Greek alphabet ending
32. Swede who had 350 patents
34. Less bountiful
39. Leaves high and dry
40. She sang "To Sir With Love"
45. Etchings, paintings, etc.
47. Communicates online

48. Horned herbivores
49. Chinese secret society
53. Lets stand, editorially
54. "Famous" cookie pioneer
55. Of sound mind
56. Ballfield covering
57. Havana hi
58. Genesis location
59. Yoga class pads
62. Stephen of "Stuck"
63. Do a seedy job?

Answers on page 187.

MUSIC

ACROSS
1. "The Prisoner of ___"
6. Aphrodite's beau
10. Mishaps for QBs
14. Fugard's "A Lesson from ___"
15. Epic chronicle
16. German "nine"
17. Singer of "You're So Vain"
19. Bite-size appetizer
20. Espionage double agents
21. More tightly drawn
23. Speeding along
25. "Happy" singer
27. "Air Music" composer Ned
28. Non-pro sports org.
29. Get under one's skin
30. Non-pro sports org.
31. Stable hand of yore
33. "To Pimp a Butterfly" rapper
38. Not exactly a thrill
39. Old office note-takers
41. Botanist's field
45. Astronaut Grissom
47. Eur. defense assn.
48. Singer nicknamed "Pearl"
52. Sailor, slangily
53. Like freelance work, often
54. Hemingway's "___ Time"
56. Give a grade to
57. The last few weeks, say
62. Zoologist Fossey
63. Doesn't last forever
64. The Who rock opera
65. Baltic states, once: Abbr.
66. Mae or Nathanael
67. Follow as a consequence

DOWN
1. Actor Efron
2. Old music note
3. Oscar-winning Sally Field role
4. "Back to the Future" car
5. Place of refuge
6. "No returns on this item"
7. Aries' animal
8. Diva's problem
9. Christmas drop-in?
10. One by one
11. Straighten up
12. Elvis's Mississippi birthplace
13. All tangled up
18. Capitol Hill VIP
22. Biblical landfall location
23. "Prince Valiant" son
24. Metronome sound
25. Fix hastily and temporarily
26. Bruce Banner's alter ego
28. Crumbly Italian cheese
31. NBA's Magic, on scoreboards
32. Golf star Ernie

34. Early data storage software
35. Pieces on chessboards
36. Lemon and melon, e.g.
37. Former newspaper section
40. Cry noisily
41. Norwegian coast features
42. Polynesian porches
43. Auto safety/tracking system
44. Matures on the vine
46. Most crafty

49. Eddie Bauer rival
50. Homey hostel
51. "Buona ___" (Italian sign-off)
55. Brush ___ (review)
58. Compass dir. near 2 o'clock
59. Audiophile's collection
60. Church-founded Dallas sch.
61. Rope on a ship

Answers on page 187.

ROBERTS RULES

ACROSS

1. Pepper grinder
5. Warner _____
9. "Dig in!"
12. Cruising
13. Spring
14. Travel itinerary letters
15. Nora Roberts romance novel
17. "Golly!"
18. Kind of sloth
19. Pass along
21. "Are you a good witch ___ bad witch?"
22. Theme park attraction
23. "Big" fast-food order
26. Little Sheba's creator
28. First-century Roman empo-rer
31. Nora Roberts romance novel
34. World's fair
35. "My Left Foot" setting
36. Otolaryngologist's abbr.
37. Temporary pause
39. Matterhorn, e.g.
41. Farsi speaker
43. Freshwater food fish
47. Plaything
48. Nora Roberts romance novel
50. Eden evictee
51. Cad
52. Letter opener
53. Mal de _____
54. Imitated
55. Periodic table fig.

DOWN

1. Schooner part
2. The Beatles' " _____ Her Standing There"
3. Late-night funnyman
4. ___-ovo-vegetarian
5. Marlene Dietrich film (with "The")
6. Perused
7. Paddle
8. "Heidi" author
9. Keen observer
10. Length X width
11. Deuce topper
16. Japanese gateway
20. "Giant" author Ferber
22. Learned anew
23. Partner for M.
24. City north of Marseilles
25. iPod alternative
27. Touch-tone trio
29. Harry Potter's friend _____ weasley

30. Not home
32. It may be proper
33. Famous lawyer Melvin
38. Nora Roberts' birth sign
40. Bamboo eater
41. Tabloid couple

42. Move aimlessly
43. Loyal
44. Painter Mondrian
45. Words from an optimist
46. Prefix with space
49. "Alley _____"

 Answers on page 187.

FANCY PARTY ATTIRE

ACROSS
1. "_____ Lazy River"
4. Stick (out)
7. With "Little" in front and 50-Across after, fancy party attire for a woman
12. Prefix with practice
13. Whichever
14. Mighty peculiar
15. Heat unit, briefly
16. Former Soviet space station
17. What 16-Across landed in after being brought down
18. Canyon edge
19. Woman's hosiery for a fancy party
21. Actress Hathaway of "The Devil Wears Prada"
23. River inlet
24. Stargazer's club: abbr.
25. Peas, in Paris
27. Woman's shoulder wrap for a fancy party
32. Do harvesting
33. Roll call vote in favor
34. XXX x X
35. River to the North Sea
37. Woman's footwear for a fancy party
43. Chaucer's far

44. "Pitfall" platform
45. "Wayne's World" denial
46. Boxer Laila, daughter of Muhammad
47. Attach again, as a brooch
48. Like some wine
49. _____ room (play area)
50. See 7-Across
51. Gender
52. Epoch of history

DOWN
1. Eclipse shadow
2. Green films
3. Women's school graduates
4. Impromptu jazz sessions
5. Apartment or condo, e.g.
6. First-timer
7. Inclined to reading and study
8. St. _____ (Caribbean island nation)
9. The sun, in ancient Egypt
10. Rugged rock formation
11. Ranges of knowledge
20. Like new dollar bills
22. Atty.'s title
25. Pie serving
26. Man-mission link
28. Street scamps
29. Sailor's assent

30. A person's fortunes
31. Office gizmo for making tags
34. Tennis great Evert
36. "All My Children" vixen
37. Challenging

38. Fusion energy org.
39. Be slack-jawed
40. Finishes
41. Oral history
42. The Underworld's boundary

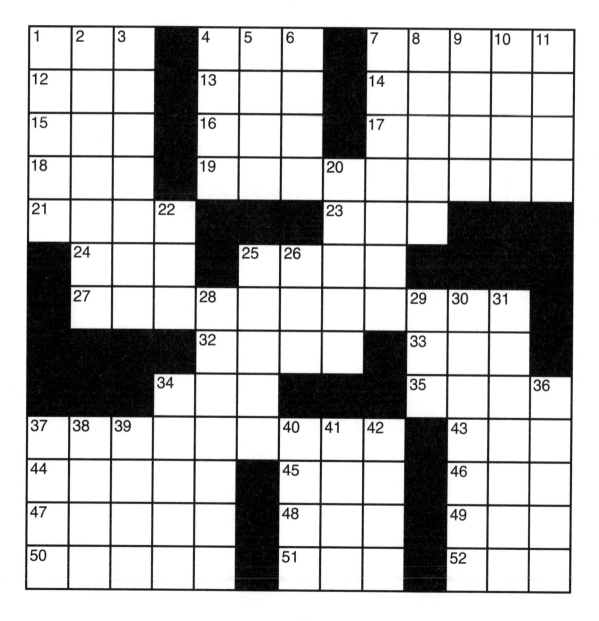

Answers on page 187.

ANCHORWOMEN

ACROSS

1. With 5-Down, amazing shot in golf
5. "Picnic" playwright
9. Played the first card
12. Middle Eastern country bordered by Turkey
13. Undercover cop
14. Mimic
15. Entrée list
16. Obama's _____ Office
17. New York's Tappan _____ Bridge
18. ABC evening news anchorwoman
21. Palm Springs-to-Las Vegas dir.
22. Pizzeria offering
23. Bored with life
26. With 33-Across, pioneering network news anchorwoman
30. Dined
31. King in a Steve Martin song
32. House member: abbr.
33. See 26-Across
36. Filler between O and U
38. Styled after
39. Lepton particle
40. CBS evening news anchor-woman
45. Birds-feather connector
46. Blacken on a grill
47. Christmas song
50. Team supporter
51. Gull's cousin
52. Birthday bakery buy
53. Rub the wrong way
54. Backtalk
55. Former spouses

DOWN

1. That guy
2. Salem's state: abbr.
3. Touch down
4. Like horses or zebras
5. See 1-Across
6. Pew location
7. Try to get
8. Slim cream puff
9. Nonindustrious
10. Sharp-bladed fencing sword
11. De Niro's "The _____ Hunter"
19. "Then what?"
20. Blogger's milieu
23. Bone or breaker beginner
24. _____ moment's notice
25. Neighbor of Md.
26. Crosstown transportation
27. Sheet music abbr.

28. Hi-_____ monitor
29. City dweller's rental: abbr.
31. Windpipe
34. _____ chi
35. Votes into office
36. Equal level
37. Pear-shaped fruit used in
    preserves

39. Changes course
40. Diplomat Annan
41. Miles away
42. Heavy-metal machine
43. Rowing poles
44. Sweet-talk
48. Scratch (out), as a living
49. "_____ Miserables"

Answers on page 187.

JUST SHOE ME

ACROSS

1. Doorway side
5. Fashionable shoes for Carrie Bradshaw
12. Middle Eastern dish
13. Magic potions
14. In worse health
15. Leaves the union
16. Style of shoes
18. Mobile's state: abbr.
19. "That's incredible!"
22. Comfortable, casual footwear
26. Lab eggs
27. "_____ got you covered"
28. Furnish with more weapons
31. U.S. anthem writer
32. Clearasil target
33. Comfortable casual shoes
35. Burns and Norton
36. There are eight in a gal.
37. Fashionable shoes for Nina Van Horn
44. Cleaning compound
47. All smiles
48. Grind _____ (slow down and stop)
49. Great Lakes Indians
50. Style of shoes
51. Went too fast

DOWN

1. Nursery rhyme tumbler
2. Sheryl Crow's "_____ Wanna Do"
3. Priestess of Dionysus
4. Thief
5. Small plateau
6. Smart guy?
7. Shaving mishap
8. Big oafs
9. Tupperware top
10. Lode deposit
11. Leaky noise
12. Rockford and Magnum, for example
17. Christian of "The Dark Knight"
19. Stopped sleeping
20. Above
21. Methods
22. 8 EEE, say, for a shoe
23. Gung-ho
24. New Jersey basketball team
25. _____ Paradise, narrator of "On the Road"
29. Thickly fibrous
30. Fire starters
34. Half step below G
37. WWE's Cena
38. _____ the buzzer

39. Venus de _____
40. Chess ending
41. Mayberry lad
42. Newspaper opinion page
43. The "S" in CBS: abbr.

44. Dave Matthews's record label
45. Do the floor
46. Fannie follower

Answers on page 187.

FUNNY FEMALES

ACROSS

1. Spoken
5. Dickensian pseudonym
8. "Citizen Kane" prop
12. Brain section
13. South Australian capital
15. Original SNL cast member
17. Beautifies
18. First vice president
19. African grazer
20. Light brown shade
22. Coach Parseghian
24. Wander about
26. Layered hairdo
30. British comedienne
33. Fencing tool
34. Accomplishments
35. Samantha of "The Daily Show"
36. Alcott's Jo, for one
38. Whirlpool bath
40. Conspires with
43. Spiritual awakening?
46. Former cohost of "The View"
49. Bus passenger's request
50. Notable times
51. Like a bug in a rug
52. Service charge
53. Diane of "Unfaithful"

DOWN

1. Spanish stewpot
2. "The _____ Not Taken"
3. Nullify
4. Acquire knowledge
5. Forbids
6. Honorific poem
7. Buddhist sect
8. Wood particles
9. Andean capital
10. Dutch treat?
11. Wolf lairs
14. "Maude" producer Norman
16. Harden
20. Make leave
21. Unit of change
22. Versatile blackjack card
23. Sound heard at 43-Across
25. Algerian port in Camus's "The Plague"
27. "Carmen" highlight
28. Noshed
29. Expletive heard on "Leave It to Beaver"
31. Winter expense
32. City of the Ruhr Valley
37. Applications
39. Board of experts
40. Buchwald and Garfunkel

41. "_____ to Run" (Springsteen hit)
42. Biblical name that means "hairy"
43. Achy
44. "Braveheart" group
45. "Anything _____" (2003 Woody Allen film)
47. Switch position
48. Emmy winner Ruby

1	2	3	4		5	6	7		8	9	10	11
12					13		14					
15			16									
17							18					
	19				20	21						
22	23			24	25				26	27	28	29
30			31				32					
33				34					35			
			36	37				38	39			
40	41	42				43				44	45	
46				47	48							
49								50				
51				52				53				

Answers on page 188.

MELTS IN YOUR MOUTH

ACROSS

1. Punching tool
4. Slightest noise
8. "Holy crow!"
12. Falsify
13. It's loaded
14. "Whip It" band
15. Schubert's "Symphony No. 8 _____ Minor"
16. Fresh out of the oven
18. Mark Twain's final resting place
20. Too weird
21. Resale site
22. Airline until 2001: abbr.
24. Three-foot units: abbr.
25. Long-time letter turner
29. Place to play video games
30. Peruvian animals
34. 2008 Sean Penn role
36. "No ___" ("I give up," in Spain)
39. Prefix with graphic
40. Jazz singer Fitzgerald
41. System matching characters to numbers, in computing: abbr.
43. Kin of "Aye, captain!"
46. Word that can follow the last words of 16-, 25-, and

34-Across
48. German article
50. Where you always are?
51. Stunned beyond words
52. Take advantage of
53. Singles
54. Female warrior of TV
55. Work with thread

DOWN

1. Actress MacGraw
2. Place to get a rose
3. Actor Matt of "Friends"
4. Spanish slang for father
5. Middle East leader
6. Person who senses others' emotions, in sci-fi
7. Hawaiian dish made from taro
8. Border
9. Architect Frank
10. Refrain from
11. Bestows excessive attention (on)
17. Satisfying way for things to be explained
19. Chatty bird
21. Longoria Parker of "Desperate Housewives"
23. Trick
26. Classical musician's "slowly"

126

27. "If I ___ a Rich Man"
28. Surname of designer couple Charles and Ray
31. Domains
32. Bailiff's command
33. Reggae relative
35. Explorer's expedition
36. Fueled by testosterone
37. Visibly shocked
38. "Jackpot!"

42. Seals (the deal)
44. Where "Shakespeare in Love" was partially filmed
45. Video game company that released the unsuccessful Dreamcast console
47. Laid-back
49. Word advertisers frequently use

Answers on page 188.

GENE KELLY

ACROSS

1. Bachelor's place
4. Genetic letters
7. Anjou or Bosc
11. Sash tied in back
12. China neighbor
13. Janis's comic strip mate
14. "_____ Girls" (1957 Gene Kelly film)
15. Freeze front?
16. "The Happy _____" (1957 Gene Kelly film)
17. Gene Kelly's partner in "Singin' in the Rain"
20. Wife or husband
22. "_____ sad but true"
23. Astringent stuff
24. [As written]
25. Frozen dessert
28. Gene Kelly's costar in "Singin' in the Rain"
32. Likely to catch on quickly
33. ISP with a circle-in-a-triangle logo
34. "My Name Is _____" (TV series)
35. 60 secs.
36. Novelist Charlotte
38. Gene Kelly's partner in "Summer Stock"

42. Cut _____
43. Car that has seen better days
44. "On _____ Little Houseboat" (Gene Kelly/Shirley MacLaine duet)
47. Notion
48. Duplex or studio
49. Ryder Cup team
50. Temporary pause
51. Keatsian "always"
52. Pro _____ (for now)

DOWN

1. Washington type
2. Maggie Simpson's grandpa
3. Reduce in price
4. Emulate Gene Kelly
5. Portrayer of Mr. Big on "Sex and the City"
6. Eastern
7. "An American in _____" (1951 Gene Kelly musical)
8. Arrow shooter of myth
9. Alack's partner
10. Needled
12. Boys
18. "3:10 to _____"
19. "Little Caesar" nickname
20. Tony winner Thompson
21. Fall heavily

24. The Sun
25. Intermittently at home, say
26. Bud of "Harold and Maude"
27. First name in legal fiction
29. "Mare's _____" (gun on "Wanted: Dead or Alive")
30. Talk show giant Phil
31. Broadway light gas
35. "For Me and _____" (Gene Kelly's first movie)
36. Betsy _____, Gene Kelly's first wife
37. Mesmerized
38. Hoosegow
39. Language written in Persian-Arabic letters
40. Fight with Gene Kelly in "The Three Musketeers"
41. French director Clair
45. Customary practice
46. Ewe mate

Answers on page 188.

THE DRESS

ACROSS

1. Hair application
4. Dog annoyance
8. Insult, figuratively
12. Org. for docs
13. Get, as rewards
14. Totally uncool
15. Ending for beat or neat
16. Gp. that published Modern Maturity
17. Everything
18. Classic folk song
21. Antlered beast
22. Lumberjack's chopper
23. Southern stew staple
25. Spend
26. Place to crash
29. Clandestine cover
33. "Affirmative"
34. _____-mo
35. Sometimes it's enough
36. H. Rider Haggard novel
37. Breakfast
38. Chaotic one, figuratively
44. San _____, Calif.
45. Beasts on the Oregon Trail
46. It has horns and a beard
47. Alan of "The West Wing"
48. Lower arm bone
49. Funny
50. It's used to pick up birdseed
51. Julia's "Ocean's Eleven" role
52. "Bill _____, the Science Guy"

DOWN

1. Group of friends
2. Arab bigwig
3. Buffalo is on it
4. Honest
5. Open fields
6. "My Name Is _____"
7. Calm down
8. Work really, really hard
9. Past curfew
10. Andy's partner on the air
11. Many collect its dispensers
19. Israeli carrier
20. Suit, for short
23. Sex ed cells
24. Critical
25. Army entertainment org.
26. Prominent shape in Arlington
27. Duke's conference: abbr.
28. Salon supply
30. Workplace inspectors: sbbr.
31. Left the yard, as a home run
32. Crowd's approval
36. Tiptoe
37. Cone-shaped lab heaters
38. One might read for it

39. Beef inspectors: abbr.
40. Toll unit
41. Yearnings
42. Harrison Ford

hero, for short
43. Subject of some paintings
44. Insult

Answers on page 188.

TRIPLE CROWN

ACROSS

1. Copier paper purchase
5. Bikini part
8. _____ Gehrig, Triple Crown winner in 1934
11. Minimal effort
12. Has a bug
14. Clip-_____ (some bow ties)
15. Triple Crown winner in 1966
18. Like yarns or webs
19. Source of poi
20. Feeling of rage
22. Toil away
26. "Eureka!"
29. Way out there
30. Like the Sahara
31. With 33-Across, Triple Crown winner in 1956
33. See 31-Across
35. Ms. Brockovich
36. _____ Paese cheese
37. _____ Francisco (NL city since 1958)
38. Roomy auto
40. Bug in a hobby farm
41. Maker of the first all-rubber basketball
43. Home to most of Turkey
47. Triple Crown winner in 1922 and 1925
52. Santa _____ winds
53. Inheritors of the Earth, in the Bible
54. _____ podrida (spicy stew)
55. _____ Williams, Triple Crown winner in 1942 and 1947
56. Magazine staffers: abbr.
57. "This _____ in Baseball" (FOX show)

DOWN

1. Ring official, for short
2. "Rabbit _____" (ballplayer's oversensitivity to razzing)
3. "Quickly!" on a memo
4. Waiter's handout
5. "Cheers" setting
6. One causing civil unrest
7. Jessica of "Sin City"
8. _____ Angeles (NL city since 1958)
9. Beatle bride Yoko _____
10. Adm.'s service branch
13. Knighted ones
16. Bowie's weapon
17. Ryan, who tossed seven no-hitters
21. Tampa Bay player
23. Liberal _____
24. "This Old House" host Bob
25. Biblical garden

26. Iowa State's city
27. Add to the staff
28. Etcher's fluid
32. Unprincipled sort
33. "Eight _____ Out" (1988 baseball movie)
34. Place to exchange vows
36. Soaked in the tub
39. 1961 AL batting champ _____ Cash
42. Fortune-teller's words
44. Cleveland's 2007 home

opener was called on account of this
45. Elba, Napoleon's place of exile, is one
46. "_____ was I ere I saw Elba"
47. Lab maze runner
48. Retired number worn by Ozzie Smith and Pee Wee Reese
49. _____ about (wander)
50. Gives approval to
51. Shaggy Tibetan beast

Answers on page 188.

PRETTY WOMAN

ACROSS

1. _____ Angeles
4. Bob Hoskins' role in "Hook"
8. Tabloid twosome
12. "The _____ Bully" (animated film with the voice of Julia Roberts)
13. Estate in "Gone with the Wind"
14. Artist Salvador
15. Flirty actress West
16. Pitcher's figs.
17. Getaway spot
18. 1990 Julia Roberts breakout film
21. Will Smith biopic
22. When a plane is due in: abbr.
23. He played Lt. Cohill in "She Wore a Yellow Ribbon"
26. Senseless?
29. At this moment
32. 2003 "artsy" Julia Roberts movie
35. Machine tooth
36. "_____ She Great" (2000 Bette Midler biopic)
37. "CSI" regular George
38. Buddy and Rob's co-writer, familiarly

40. Ex of Artie and Mickey
42. 1999 Julia Roberts flick with Hugh Grant
47. Gumbo pod
48. "Misery" actor James
49. "The _____ Couple"
52. Sack dress designer
53. Shrek, for instance
54. By way of
55. Tractor-trailer
56. Stated
57. Quiche base

DOWN

1. Quick flight
2. "Love _____ Rooftop"
3. Kind of stool or ladder
4. "_____ Magnolias" (1989 Julia Roberts movie)
5. Bond drinks
6. Word in a proof ending
7. Good-tempered
8. Moron
9. Island of "devils"
10. Jazz legend Fitzgerald
11. Aura or demeanor
19. _____ avis
20. Intricate patterns
23. TNT alternative
24. Oozy stuff
25. Light wavelength

134

27. "Lt. Robin Crusoe, _____"
   (1966 Disney film)
28. Spy played by Greta Garbo
30. Ancient
31. Film director Craven
33. Leslie Caron musical
34. Breakfast or supper
39. Maker of the game Aster-
   oids
41. Grew like ivy

42. Approvals
43. "Illegals" or "scum" from
   "The Grapes of Wrath"
44. Ones ranked E-4 to E-9:
   abbr.
45. Enthusiastic, to the max
46. 1996 Julia Roberts movie
   "Everyone Says I _____ You"
50. Search for buried treasure
51. Trygve's successor

Answers on page 188.

FASHION FORWARD

ACROSS
1. Wide-eyed predators
5. Lincoln and Burrows
9. Old hand, for short
12. Violent public disorder
13. Guy
14. Lamb's mother
15. Fashion designer Liz
17. Movie critic Reed
18. Confuse
19. Aviator Amelia
21. Exile isle for Napoleon
23. Tool with teeth
24. Bother persistently
27. Sightseeing trip
29. Nukes
32. Insubstantial
34. Golfer Sandra with 42 LPGA Tour wins, 1962-1982
36. In person
37. Hauled into court
39. Comprehend
40. Sense organ
42. Manicurist's focus
44. Michigan city
47. Relieves
51. "Monsters, ____"
52. Fashion designer Yves
54. To the ____ degree
55. Fast-food magnate Ray
56. Strip in the Middle East
57. Tofu source
58. Seasoning herb
59. School in England

DOWN
1. Killer whale
2. Rampant
3. Laundry unit
4. Subway entrance
5. Hubbub
6. Dresser
7. "Giant" writer Ferber
8. Prophets
9. Fashion designer known for her wedding gowns
10. Ornamental jug
11. Schoolbook
16. Trouser accessories
20. Obscured by air pollution
22. "____ on the Side" (Whoopi Goldberg film)
24. Org. of Lions and Bears
25. The Greatest
26. Fashion designer Hubert de ____
28. Perlman of "Cheers"
30. Pizza order
31. Matched group
33. Butcher's offering
35. French farewell

38. Clear a drain
41. Jeopardizes
43. Big
44. Brooches
45. Not taken in by

46. Gillette blade
48. Part of pants
49. Automaker Ferrari
50. Spider-Man creator Lee
53. High card

1	2	3	4		5	6	7	8		9	10	11
12					13					14		
15				16						17		
18						19			20			
			21		22			23				
24	25	26		27			28		29		30	31
32			33			34	35					
36					37	38				39		
		40		41		42			43			
44	45				46			47		48	49	50
51				52			53					
54				55					56			
57				58					59			

Answers on page 189.

ACROSS

1. 2009 Nobel Peace Prize winner
6. Switch position
9. Cartoon bark
12. With 55-Across, Mary with an eponymous TV show
13. Evergreen tree
14. That woman
15. River in Paris
16. Pub quaff
17. Put _____ good word for
18. "CSI" evidence
20. Fossil finder Mary
22. Impressionist painter Mary
26. Makes tea
27. Home plate official
28. Look forward to
30. Tampa body of water
31. R&B singer Mary J.
32. Runner's pace
35. Honking birds
36. Yes to Yvette
37. Spine-tingling
40. Mary of Peter, Paul and Mary
43. Mary on a Scottish throne
45. Mexican Mrs.
46. It rises at dawn
47. Chewing material
49. Of yore
53. "Much _____ About Nothing"
54. Can. neighbor
55. See 12-Across
56. Tokyo currency
57. "_____ kingdom come..."
58. Desi of Desilu

DOWN

1. NFL tiebreakers
2. "See ya!"
3. "Thrilla in Manila" boxer
4. Darns
5. Concert venue
6. Three _____ kind (poker hand)
7. Spread through
8. No-cost item
9. "Take _____!" ("Beat It!")
10. Keep one's subscription going
11. Shows wear, as old clothing
19. "_____ of Two Cities"
21. Museum display
22. Baby bear
23. Docs' org.
24. 007, for one
25. Hip-swiveling dance
29. Golden-_____ (seniors)

31. Potbelly from too many quaffs
32. Coffee, in slang
33. "It'll be _____ little secret"
34. American soldiers, for short
35. Model Carangi played by Angelina Jolie
37. Test format
38. Piano exercise
39. Like many overlong sentences
41. Bakery enticement
42. Bravery in battle
44. Rear end
48. Spring month
50. Mafia boss
51. Timeline segment
52. Pince-_____ glasses

Answers on page 189.

GIRL, BY ANOTHER NAME

ACROSS

1. Toxic compound, for short
4. Pasta variety
8. Suck air
12. Large ISP
13. Jannings of old films
14. Breakfast spread
15. Suffix with percent
16. Illegal motion by a pitcher
17. Slip through the cracks
18. Social standing associated with workers
21. Pro follower
22. "By the _____ Get to Phoenix"
26. Umpire's call
27. Excuse for tardiness
30. College web address ending
31. Behavioral pattern
32. An NCO
33. Casino city
35. Price of a ride
36. Something to lend or bend
37. Absolutely positive
38. Communion table symbol
43. Morales of "Caprica"
46. Baltic Sea tributary
47. The Buckeyes coll.
48. Humdinger
49. "When Harry Met Sally..." writer Ephron
50. Show agreement
51. "Girl, Interrupted," e.g.
52. Unappetizing food
53. Puncture sound

DOWN

1. Container for Jack and Jill
2. Someone born in Denver
3. Lost one's cool
4. Referee, slangily
5. Apple of a sort
6. Money drawer
7. Actress Chase
8. Dish up the dirt
9. Pub offering
10. Match a poker bet
11. Kind of culture
19. Summer along the Seine
20. Leave in the text
23. Coconut cookies
24. They really get steamed
25. Bikini, for one
26. Ward of "Once and Again"
27. Fall back
28. Lawyers' org.
29. Carol contraction
31. Vindictive Greek goddess
34. Medication for anxiety
35. Mink or ermine
37. Throw out

39. Half a picker-upper
40. Heartthrob
41. Pop pianist Peter
42. Beer, slangily

43. Santa's helper
44. _____ generis
45. Best effort

Answers on page 189.

PATRIOTIC CLOTHES

ACROSS

1. Many a new driver
9. Dundee dweller
13. Classic Caddy
14. Vagabond
15. Cloaked folklore heroine
17. Former big name in long distance, briefly
18. "Don't go!"
19. Korean auto
20. Inscribed pillar
23. Like fresh cake
25. Quick on the uptake
29. Honor with a party
30. Traditional headwear of good guys
32. Layer of paint
34. Fashion
35. Deodorant brand
37. Dental filling
41. Sch. for ministers
42. Pro _____ (in proportion)
46. Before, in verse
47. Literary women nicknamed for their hosiery
51. Egyptian snakes
52. On the move
53. Big name in oil
54. Connects with

DOWN

1. Contract conditions
2. Vote into office
3. Comedian Murphy
4. Neither companion
5. Former Bush spokesman Fleischer
6. Wanders for pleasure
7. Prepare copy
8. Columnist Barrett
9. "Quiet down!"
10. Snacks sold by Girl Scouts
11. Woodwind player
12. Until now
16. Workout place
21. Christine of "Chicago Hope"
22. Yale student
24. Time and again
26. Many "Star Wars" characters, briefly
27. Part of AARP: abbr.
28. "Love _____ neighbor..."
30. Exercise apparel
31. Will Smith title role
32. "Rock the _____"
33. Threat words
36. J and Dre
38. First Soviet premier
39. Trade talk

40. Binary question
43. "They're _____ again!"
44. Collette of "In Her Shoes"
45. Very top

48. Snaky shape
49. Some boxing Ws
50. "...see _____ will believe..."

1	2	3	4	5	6	7	8		9	10	11	12
13									14			
15							16					
17				18					19			
20			21	22				23	24			
		25		26	27	28		29			
	30						31				
32	33			34							
35				36			37		38	39	40
41			42	43	44	45			46		
47			48				49	50			
51				52							
53				54							

Answers on page 189.

LITTLE WOMEN

ACROSS

1. Butter portion
4. Hourly pay
8. Join in the game
12. Nest egg
13. Geometrical finding
14. Anecdotal knowledge
15. Money-saving investment
17. Pops the question
18. Car in a Beach Boys song: hyph.
19. Lounge (around)
21. Lion protest
24. Party nuts
27. Leave rolling in the aisles
30. London gallery
32. "Take on Me" band
33. Internet provider
34. Bait and tackle workers
35. Flag thrower, at times
36. Everything
37. C & W mecca, with "the"
38. Ending for Jean or Ann
39. Marshy inlet
41. Toothy tools
43. Removes with clippers
45. Without a connection
49. Tributes in verse
51. Chocolate snack
54. German auto
55. Computer operator
56. Life story
57. Door openers
58. "Hour" actor Omar
59. Aardvark entree

DOWN

1. "12 Monkeys" actor Brad
2. A Middle East inhabitant
3. Travel across a tarmac
4. Ralph _____ Emerson
5. Sculptures and such
6. "That's incredible!"
7. Jason Lee's "My Name is _____"
8. Town square
9. Becomes discouraged
10. Boat for pairs
11. "That's right!"
16. Fortified wine
20. WWII pilots
22. Money for the server
23. Bacon servings
25. Sharpen, as a knife
26. Partner for sound
27. Sad-sounding auto?
28. 1970 hit by The Kinks
29. "The Breakfast Club" actress
31. Glen Campbell's "_____ Little Kindness"

34. Horsemen count
38. Catch a glimpse of
40. Desert garden
42. Laundromat appliances
44. Elizabeth of "Leaving Las Vegas"
46. Swedish band

47. Drought ender
48. Moderate pace
49. Adult acorn
50. Scheduled to arrive
52. Telepathy, e.g.
53. Exercise unit

Answers on page 189.

THE IT BAG

ACROSS

1. "It bag" from Bottega Veneta
5. _____ Vegas
8. Sch. supporters
12. Western New York county
13. Unseldom
14. _____avis
15. Joyous celebration
16. TGIF portion
17. Word of woe
18. "It bag" from Balenciaga
21. "It bag" from Louis Vuitton
24. A Montague to a Capulet
25. Sidestep
26. Like the Chrysler Building
30. Rocky crag
31. "It bag" from Fendi
32. Chinese cookware
33. Temporary substitute
36. Serena's best friend on Gossip Girl
38. _____ de toilette
39. "It bag" from Kooba
40. "It bag" from Chloé
44. Money spent in Istanbul
45. "I'm _____ Sexy" (1992 Right Said Fred hit)
46. Julian McMahon's role on "Nip/Tuck"

50. Men's clothing store in SoHo
51. Diva's problem
52. Big caucus site
54. Credit card figure
54. Lambaste
55. "It bag" from Dolce and Gabbana

DOWN

1. Beer container
2. Org. with some big guns?
3. Word after snake or coconut
4. Gotten together, with "up"
5. Like some ambitions
6. _____ Samurai (cartoon)
7. Cook with a 32-Across
8. Hoped (for)
9. Main ingredient in traditional cosmetics
10. Kazakhstan's _____ Sea
11. Request from an ed.
19. Inspired poem
20. Foldout bed
21. Dinnerware collections
22. Novel element
23. Continental monetary unit
24. "Killer" PC program
27. Actor "McGregor"
28. _____ purse

146

29. Thickening agent in gumbo
31. Supermodel walk
34. Bookish one
35. _____ Mattiolo
36. Short profile
37. Soup bit
39. Urban hangout
40. Proceed wearily
41. Personal assistant
42. Small amount
43. "The Wayward Wind" singer Grant
47. Fashion designer Alice _____
48. Night bird
49. Triumphant cry

1	2	3	4		5	6	7		8	9	10	11
12					13				14			
15					16				17			
			18	19				20				
21	22	23					24					
25						26				27	28	29
30					31					32		
33			34	35				36	37			
			38				39					
40	41	42				43						
44					45				46	47	48	49
50					51				52			
53					54				55			

Answers on page 189.

CUBIC ZIRCONIA

ACROSS

1. Limber
6. RN treatment
9. Demand, as a price
12. FedEX won't deliver to one
13. Written hugs
14. On the _____ vive (watchful)
16. Vigor
18. Cleo's snake
19. Big basin
21. Les _____-Unis (the United States, in France)
22. "_____ the season..."
23. Goof up
24. Cut of cubic zirconia
28. _____ Chen shoes
31. Leave at the altar
32. Winter mo.
33. Pineapple platation island
34. The sun, personified
35. Cut of cubic zirconia
37. Calif. airport: abbr.
39. Peas' place
40. "Watch it wiggle, see it jiggle" dessert
43. Society newcomer
44. Genesis vessel
47. Cut of cubic zirconia
49. Counterindicate
51. En preceders

52. Culpa preceder
53. Like a vacuum
54. Kind of flour or whiskey
55. Cheer of a sort
56. Deceptive ploys

DOWN

1. Grp. for Nancy Lopez
2. Acknowledgements of debt
3. Cook's meas.
4. On everyone's wish list
5. Foreign
6. Pyramid, to a Pharaoh
7. Mauna _____
8. Cider-making device
9. Light greenish blue
10. Executive, slangily
11. Bride's greeting
17. Fiscal time frame: abbr.
20. Having had experience in
22. "The Closer" network
23. Getaway
24. Slumber party wear, for short
25. Spanish river
26. Not well
27. Consult
28. Glass vessel
29. "I guessed it!"
30. Rustic affirmative
33. Quaint

36. Robin Hood, for one
37. Camera type: abbr.
38. Lather-laden
40. Fan's disapproval
41. TV award
42. _____ majesty (act of treason)
43. WWII milestone
44. Swiss peaks
45. Solemn act
46. Custodian's jinglers
48. Actress Thompson
50. Flightless fowl in the outback

Answers on page 190.

CELEBS WITH TWINS

ACROSS

1. Cold and damp, as a dungeon
5. Abates
9. Part of a rustic address
12. Turkey neighbor
13. _____ le monde (everybody)
14. "The Fresh Prince of Bel _____"
15. Actress with twins Dolly and Charlie
18. Electrical weapon
19. Trucker's commincation
20. British actor Jude
22. Part of a min.
23. England's Queen _____
26. Part of Tina Turner's outfit
28. Bee's home
32. Actress with twins Knox and Vivienne
36. Robin Cook thriller
37. A, in Amiens
38. Phat Fashions director Kimora _____ Simmons
39. Bare mountain peak
42. Co. acquired by American Airlines in 2001
44. "_____ and Old Lace"
48. Awards ceremony host
52. Singer-actress with twins Max and Emme
54. Legal org.
55. Word following Ye in some shops
56. Colombian city
57. _____ & Bone
58. Require
59. _____ buco (veal dish)

DOWN

1. It's dished by gossip columnists
2. Kind of rug
3. Kidnaps
4. Prepare for knighthood
5. Mail Boxes _____
6. Old U.K. airline
7. Eccentric Tom Hanks comedy, with "The"
8. Mall unit
9. _____ someone's closet
10. Bottled water brand
11. Sean Connery's first Bond movie
16. Swimming stroke
17. Far from effete
21. _____ Fit
23. Cosmetics firm
24. Hair product by Orlando Bloom
25. Roaring lion studio

27. African antelope
29. Not well
30. Compete
31. Big foot meas.
33. Consumed
34. Picnic raider
35. "Intuition" singer
40. French _____ soup
41. Winchester product
43. British Petroleum partner

44. Almost closed
45. Sitcom starring a country singer
46. Hosiery trouble
47. Surrender, as land
49. H&R Block employees
50. Slithery swimmers
51. He played Emile in "South Pacific"
53. Crimson or cherry

Answers on page 190.

APPLIANCE ATTACHMENTS

ACROSS

1. Hearty swallow
5. Regret bitterly
8. Little green edibles
12. Pisa's river
13. Mounds of insects
15. Guy that makes breakfast?
17. Unrestrained shopping
18. Flow out
19. Bach instrument
22. Watering hole
26. Seminary subject
28. Lying over something
30. Horne of music
31. Stolen pane?
34. _____ about
35. He watched Rome burn
36. "Piggy" on a tot's foot
37. Willem of "Spiderman"
39. Often poisonous plant
41. High school equivalency
43. Save on wedding bills
46. Wandering cook?
51. No one
52. Pilot's post
53. Prune, before dying
54. NBC sketch show
55. Type of code

DOWN

1. Toothy tools
2. Scarf or shawl
3. Facing
4. Errand runner
5. Comic actress Charlotte
6. Prefix with corn
7. French I verb
8. Arcade game
9. Spreading tree
10. Menu phrase
11. IRS info
14. Vagabond
16. By-the-book
20. Words before impasse
21. Do, re and mi
23. Upholstery protector
24. _____ many words
25. Request from an ed.
26. Did blacksmith work
27. New Rochelle college
29. Lima's nation
32. Playbill
33. First name in Mayberry
38. Pitcher stats
40. Honolulu hello
42. Eve's grandson
44. Brazilian booter
45. Humorist Bombeck
46. Total U.S. output, e.g.
47. Internet provider letters
48. Early Beatle Sutcliffe

49. Rev
50. Conduit bend

1	2	3	4		5	6	7		8	9	10	11
12					13			14				
15				16								
17							18					
	19			20	21		22		23	24	25
26	27			28		29		30			
31			32				33				
34					35					36		
37				38		39			40			
		41		42			43			44	45
46	47	48				49	50				
51								52			
53				54				55			

Answers on page 190.

VIDEO FAVES

ACROSS

1. Strikebreaker
5. Beetle juice?
8. IRS functionaries: abbr.
12. Sling the mud
13. "Rhoda" mom
14. "_____ Williams" (1985 movie)
15. Hall-of-Famer Boggs
16. Pen-point'
17. Chemical compound
18. "Girl, Interrupted" actress
21. "No" vote
22. TV's "American _____"
23. "_____ is Born" (1976 film)
26. "General Hospital" roles
27. Boston Bruins legend Bobby
30. "Rocket Man" singer Elton
31. Inlet
32. Film-rating organization: abbr.
33. Prop for the Tin Man
34. "The Hunt for _____ October" (1990 thriller)
35. "Blue _____ Shoes: Elvis Presley song
36. BBC, familiarly
38. Cardinal's cap insignia: abbr.
39. "Couples Retreat" star
43. Hoedown setting
44. "Vaya _____ Dios"
45. Be a bookworm
47. "Me, Myself _____" Vitamin C hit
48. New England cape
49. Goddess of strife
50. "Touched by and Angel" angel
51. Singer Winehouse
52. Poet Whitman

DOWN

1. 202.50 degrees on the compass
2. Lobster feature
3. German car
4. Eileen in "Murder by Death"
5. Rob Weasley's sister
6. Sarah McLachlan hit
7. Witchy Melissa Joan Hart role
8. Philosophy
9. Cruz in "Elegy"
10. Love deity
11. Roman sun god
19. Sampan mover
20. NFL rushing stats: abbr.
23. Steely Dan album
24. Boston team, for short
25. 1963 Hitchcock film

26. Weed out
28. "Cool!"
29. _____ Dawn Chong of "Quest for Fire"
31. Kirstie's "Cheers" role
32. Kate of "Star Trek: Voyager"
34. Part of R&R: abbr.
35. Disco _____ of "The Simpsons"
37. "Brokeback Mountain" cowboy
38. "Grease" heroine
39. Wind indicator
40. "Va-va-_____!"
41. Olympian queen
42. "Hammer and _____ " Indigo Girls song
43. Dracula, on occasion
46. Summer time: abbr.

Answers on page 190.

COUNTRY FOLK

ACROSS
1. Applaud
5. Sort
8. "Hairspray" stage mother
12. Ring up
13. Moo goo _____ pan
14. "Nobody _____ It Better": Simon
15. Philbin's co-host
16. Polish coat of arms
17. Rolled sandwich
18. "Tim McGraw" singer
21. "So long, Guiseppe!"
22. Near eternity
23. Mr./Mrs. played by Pitt and Jolie
25. Johnson in "Tooth Fairy"
30. Feel malaise
31. Bridal party
35. "The Bridges of Madison _____" (1995 movie)
38. Nobel-winning UN agency: abbr.
39. Williams of country music fame
40. "9 to 5" singer
44. "Physician, _____ thyself"
45. "The Greatest" boxer
46. "Twins" director Reitman
48. Hawaiian menu fish, for short
49. _____ Lonely Boys
50. "_____ Kleine Nachtmusik"
51. Burden
52. Rock's Third _____ Blind
53. Sing like Ella Fitzgerald

DOWN
1. "Proud Mary" band, for short
2. Café au _____
3. "Scent of a Woman" star
4. "_____ to the Bone" (1999 film)
5. Arctic adobes
6. Simba's shelter
7. "('Til) I _____ You": Everly Brothers
8. Mrs. Doubtfire
9. Tim Conway character
10. Apple-pie order
11. Horned ciper
19. "Well, _____-di-dah"
20. "Holy cow!"
23. Maggie, to Jake Gyllenhaal
24. _____-jongg
26. "Amish Paradise" singer Al
27. Minor carp
28. British cathedral city
32. Bruce in "Live Free or Die Hard"

33. Added wing
34. "Casino _____" (2006 Bond film)
35. Sunbather's chair
36. Gondola mover
37. Loosens

40. James in "East of Eden"
41. Kauai's neighbor
42. Artifice
43. Granny
44. Medical insurane plan: abbr.
47. Volleyball mesh

1	2	3	4		5	6	7		8	9	10	11
12					13				14			
15					16				17			
	18			19				20				
		21					22					
23	24						25			26	27	28
29										30		
31			32	33	34		35	36	37			
			38				39					
	40	41				42					43	
44					45				46			47
48					49				50			
51					52				53			

Answers on page 190.

ON THE SCREEN

ACROSS
1. "A Bug's Life" bugs
5. Morgan Freeman's "Bruce Almighty" role
8. Slightly open
12. Sing like Ella
13. Gardner in "The Naked Maja"
14. Emulate Earhart
15. "Elizabeth: The Golden Age" star
18. Israeli seaport
19. World holder
20. Chick-_____-A Bowl
22. Zany comedian Phiips
23. "The Seven Year Itch" star
30. Part of MYOB
31. _____ Hudson in "Cars"
32. "Shallow _____" (2001)
33. 1961 folm that won 10 Oscars
38. Acting coach Hagen
39. Archaic verb suffix
40. Winger in "Urban Cowboy"
43. Eagle nest
47. "Message to Michael" singer
51. "Rule, Britannia!" composer
52. Old Navy's parent
53. "Amazing Grace" ending
54. Sinatra's "It Was a Very Good _____"
55. Maned antelope
56. Scrabble 10-pointers

DOWN
1. "The Nazarene" author Sholem
2. Rose Bowl organization: abbr.
3. Jacques in "Mon Oncle"
4. Graf of tennis
5. "The Sleepy Time _____" (2001 film)
6. Gametes
7. Aykroyd in "1941"
8. Kutcher in "What Happens in Vegas"
9. Ehtan Coen's brother
10. Utah ski spot
11. Spoils
16. Get-out-of-jail money
17. Hunter's garb, slangily
21. Debbue Allen's "Fame" role
22. Show host
23. Groom a fairway
24. Shock partner
25. "General Hospital" roles
26. "Yes" gesture
27. 17th Greek letter
28. Henley crewman

29. Tarzan actor Ron
34. Kathleen in "Peggy Sue Got Married"
35. Comic book Pionner Lee
36. Oscar presenter
37. "Ease on Down the Road" musical
40. "Saving Private Ryan" date

41. Emerald Isle
42. _____fide
44. Greet the judge
45. Burger King drink
46. Barely gets (by)
48. Prairie oyster
49. Obi-_____ Kenobi
50. Kwik-E-Mart proprietor

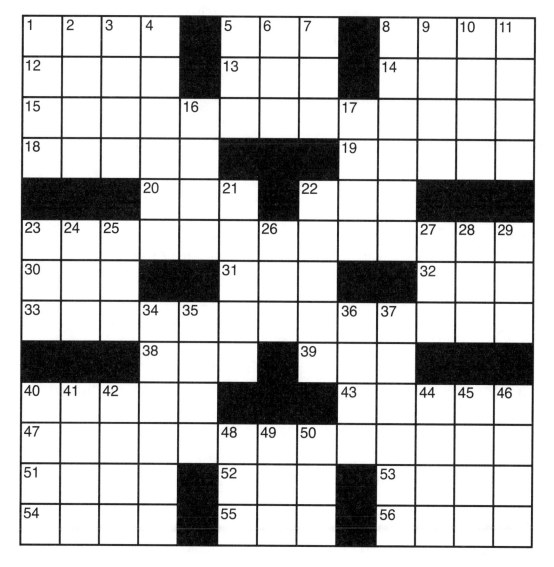

Answers on page 190.

STAR APPEAL

ACROSS

1. Draped drapery
5. "Cold Mountain" heroine
8. 2004 Brad Pitt film
12. Banjoist Scruggs
13. High-jump hurdle
14. Taken-back item, for short
15. The Dixie Chicks, e.g.
16. Consumed
17. Sandler in "Anger Manage-ment"
18. Reality show with judges
21. Letters of debt
22. "Entourage" agent
23. Vacuums or dusts
26. Bullock in "Speed"
30. Acorn sources
31. Score for Mia Hamm
32. Algonquian abode
35. Lanvin perfume
37. Before now
38. "Erie Canal" mule
39. "Rachel Getting Married" star
45. Places for sweaters?
46. Atmosphere
47. Miracle site in John 2:1
48. Atlantic City game
49. Bachelor's last words
50. Earth Day subject: abbr.
51. Persia now
52. Legal point
53. Acoustic unit

DOWN

1. Bristle
2. Summery
3. "Beautiful Flower" singer India _____
4. Cinematic "Sunset Boule-vard" star
5. Beaded counter
6. "Star Trek: TNG" android
7. Sites for sporting matches
8. Dan Aykroyd/Eddie Murphy film
9. Makeover
10. Translucent gem
11. _____ Kippur
19. Saturn model
20. Hayes in "Flags of Our Fa-thers"
23. Gateway's mascot
24. "Love Story" composer Francis
25. Cardiogram
27. Stag's mate
28. "Maple Leaf _____": Joplin
29. Nut-brown drink
33. "The _____ of Innocence" (1993 film)

34. Angora fabric
35. Houston ball club
36. Super Bowl Sunday sound
39. Mimic
40. Wendy's St. Bernard

41. Adjutant
42. Baylor's city
43. Soon
44. Whiffenpoof Society school
45. Aprés-_____ party

1	2	3	4		5	6	7		8	9	10	11
12					13				14			
15					16				17			
18				19			20					
			21			22						
23	24	25				26			27	28	29	
30								31				
32			33	34		35	36					
		37			38							
	39	40			41				42	43	44	
45				46				47				
48				49				50				
51				52				53				

Answers on page 191.

THRILLERS

ACROSS
1. Mary's pet
5. L.A. summer hours: abbr.
8. Lance Armstrong's bike brand
12. Grandpa Munster's pet
13. Chop down
14. 2009 Beyoncé hit
15. "Scat!"
16. Baboon
17. "_____ Almighty"
18. "Beverly Hills 90210" producer
21. Hakeem _____-Kazim in "Hotel Rwanda"
22. Leoni in "Flying Blind"
23. "What's My Line?" mystery
26. Big Bird's street
30. Vigoda and Beame
31. Streetcar
32. Singer Vandross
35. Voice of Mr. Magoo, Jim _____
37. _____ de France
38. CC Sabathia stat: abbr.
39. "Notorious" actress
46. TV's "Saved by the _____"
47. Morse E
48. Neophyte
49. Praise
50. Fangorn Forest dweller
51. "QB VII" author Uris
52. "Desire Under the _____" (1958 film adaptation)
53. Scheider in "Jaws"
54. Falco in "The Sopranos"

DOWN
1. "The Simpsons" saxophonist
2. Ottoman leader
3. Othello, for one
4. "Suddenly Susan" star
5. Star Fleet weapon
6. 2009 Dillinger portrayer, Johnny
7. Twitter posts
8. 2001 Robert Redford film
9. Sitarist Shankar
10. Flair
11. "King _____" (2005)
19. Scots denial
20. Jason of "My Name Is Earl"
23. Oriole great Ripken
24. "Aladdin" monkey
25. No longer working: abbr.
27. "Raiders of the Lost _____" (1981)
28. Egyptian _____ cat
29. Ambulance letters
33. Annex

34. 2008 Kate Winslet film, with "The"
35. Warren _____ in "Bonnie and Clyde"
36. _____ gratia artis
39. Up to the task
40. Newman's "Hud" costar Patricia
41. Morose
42. U2 frontman
43. Van Morrison's "Brown _____ Girl"
44. Deanna of "Star Trek: TNG"
45. Rapper _____-Loc

1	2	3	4		5	6	7		8	9	10	11
12					13				14			
15					16				17			
18				19				20				
			21				22					
23	24	25					26			27	28	29
30									31			
32				33	34		35	36				
			37				38					
39	40	41				42				43	44	45
46					47				48			
49					50				51			
52					53				54			

Answers on page 191.

WOMEN OF ACTION

ACROSS

1. "Lara Croft: _____ Raider" (2001 movie)
5. Air-gun ammo
8. Burlap fiber
12. 1998 Sarah McLachlan hit
13. Remy in "Ratatouille"
14. Right after
15. Mardi Gras follower
16. Singer Midge
17. Adriatic resort
18. CBS drama series
21. Mandela's organization: abbr.
22. Golf ball position
23. Captain of cereal
26. Accumulate interest
30. Travel in cyberspace
31. Bicorn and tricorn
32. Block houses?
35. Meryl in "Julie & Julia"
37. "His Master's Voice" company: abbr.
38. Polynesian dish
39. Star of 18-Across
46. Regal name of Norway
47. Caviar
48. Scrabble piece
49. Birthmark
50. Favorite Favre target

51. Brainstorm
52. Look through a keyhole
53. _____ Paulo
54. Gave the once-over

DOWN

1. After-shower application
2. River to the Baltic
3. Skirt length
4. 1995 Jim Carrey film
5. Midmorning meal
6. Theda "The Vamp"
7. "A Streetcar Named Desire" role
8. "Doctor Zhivago" star
9. "Wrapped _____ You": Garth Brooks song
10. Sarah Palin's hubby
11. "Dukes of Hazzard" spinoff
19. "Monsters, _____" (2001 animated film)
20. Karaoke need, briefly
23. CBS forensic drama
24. Trapdoor concealer
25. Internet address
27. Charlotte of "The Facts of Life"
28. SUV, for short
29. Psychic's skills: abbr.
33. Witch month: abbr.
34. Buffalo wings?

35. Michael Phelps sponsor
36. Taos lift
39. Ceremonial display
40. Skin-cream additive
41. Wind of 49-50 knots

42. Gossip queen Barrett
43. Spick-and-span
44. General Robert _____
45. Pick up a book

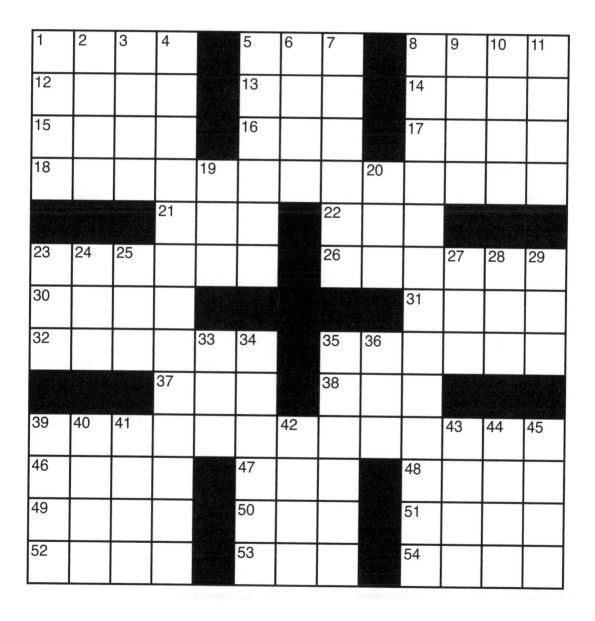

Answers on page 191.

ACROSS

1. Cuff link's spot
5. Third degree?: abbr.
8. Romanov ruler
12. Pained response
13. Like steak tartare
14. Cronyn in "The Pelican Brief"
15. Scamper
16. Had brunch
17. Beautiful race in "The Time Machine"
18. "Breakfast at Tiffany's" star
21. Wrath
22. "Akeelah and the _____" (2006 film)
23. Debra in "Rachel Getting Married"
26. Kevin in "Beyond the Sea"
30. Per unit
31. It's chained in Alaska
32. Overacts
35. "Key Largo" star Humphrey
37. Hard drinker
38. Perfect test score
39. "Oops!...I Did It Again" singer
46. Ballerina's outfit
47. Anatomical duct
48. Vaccination
49. F-16 wing letters
50. Busta Rhymes album
51. Scandinavian capital
52. Feudal slave
53. Bottom-line
54. Josh Groban Christmas album

DOWN

1. Davenport
2. "Little" girl of comics
3. Long Island _____ tea
4. 1983 film about the Mercury Seven
5. "Gloria Patri" is one
6. "Thirty days _____ ..."
7. Uncool guys
8. Sonny & Cher hit
9. "Star Trek" navigator
10. Cupid
11. Jockey's strap
19. Before, in verse
20. Get-up-and-go
23. Bitsy
24. "_____ ...Sasha Fierce": Beyoncé album
25. Sgt.
27. Leon Panetta's old agency: abbr.
28. Drop the ball
29. Nevertheless

33. Near eternity
34. Spielberg or Jobs
35. Jacqueline in "Carolina Moon"
36. Caveman of comics
39. Heat measures: abbr.
40. Tricky move

41. _____-TASS news agency
42. Ivy League school
43. "Now I get it!"
44. Portrayal
45. Short-runway plane: abbr.

Answers on page 191.

TV TRIVIA

ACROSS
1. Muslim pilgrimage
5. Masseur employer
8. Spat
12. Sunburn soother
13. Rocky crag
14. Winter coat
15. Tournament seeding
16. "Baby's Day _____" (1994 comedy)
17. French-1 verb
18. Natalie Teeger on "Monk"
21. Triangle side
22. Mystifier Geller
23. Sobieski in "Joan of Arc"
26. Gave a Bronx cheer
30. Utah ski spot
31. River into Lake Biel
32. Place for a food basket
35. Fairchild on "Falcon Crest"
37. Homer's "Stupid Me!"
38. Provincetown cape
39. 1983 Meryl Streep film
46. Colorful parrot
47. Amtrak guesstimate: abbr.
48. Subway token
49. New Jersey Nets' home
50. Six, in Venice
51. 2008 John Cusack animated film
52. Cartoon skunk Le Pew
53. Suffix for east
54. Groggy: alt.

DOWN
1. Johnny who drew 8-Down
2. Old orchard spray
3. Lady of Spain
4. Long-running 1997 Broadway musical
5. Larry, Curly, or Moe
6. Rain cats and dogs
7. Bea of "Maude"
8. Sir Rodney's comic strip
9. Slight trace
10. Jamie of "M*A*S*H"
11. "I Love Lucy" landlord
19. Linda _____ (Supergirl)
20. _____ pro nobis
23. Indy 500 unit
24. Manning of N.Y. Giants
25. List-ending: abbr.
27. Zig partner
28. _____ of Good Feeling
29. Place for a TV
33. "_____ Dalmatians" (1961 animated film)
34. Roquefort, for one
35. Palin's 2008 running mate
36. Marvel aloud
39. Petticoat

40. Soft mud
41. Yorick's skull, for one
42. Gang followr
43. Othello's ensign

44. Riding whip
45. Like a Stephen King tale: var.

1	2	3	4	■	5	6	7	■	8	9	10	11
12				■	13			■	14			
15				■	16			■	17			
18				19				20				
■	■		21			■	22			■	■	■
23	24	25				■	26			27	28	29
30			■	■	■	■	■	31				
32				33	34	■	35	36				
■	■		37			■	38			■	■	■
39	40	41				42			■	43	44	45
46				■	47			■	48			
49				■	50			■	51			
52				■	53			■	54			

Answers on page 191.

LEADING AMYS

ACROSS

1. Tread heavily
6. Laura Bush's alma mater: abbr.
9. Completely
12. Peter of "The Maltese Falcon"
13. Beer container
14. Actress Farrow
15. "Yentl" costar
17. Up until now
18. County singer Williams or Ritter
19. Neill or Nunn
20. Bicker
22. Be the right size
23. Part of ACLU: abbr.
24. Singing syllables
27. Disentangle
30. Peruvian capital
31. The theme of this puzzle
32. Med student's subject: abbr.
33. Islands near Jamaica
35. Mink's playful cousin
36. Up to the job
37. Place for a mud bath
38. West Point student
40. Meadow
41. Mining excavation
44. Nest-egg investment option: abbr.
45. She played Dr. Coburn on "ER"
48. Director Burton
49. Christianity or Buddhism: abbr.
50. Loan-sharking
51. Harris and O'Neill
52. Sault _____ Marie: abbr.
53. Relaxes

DOWN

1. Shutter or blind part
2. Scholarly volume
3. Gemsbok
4. Medical imaging: abbr.
5. Iran, pre-1935
6. Milk choice
7. Restroom sign
8. Entertainer Leslie
9. Wife of Vince Gill
10. In _____ of
11. Tardy
16. Industrial container
21. Soprano Tebaldi
22. Set food on fire
23. Whatever
24. Mom's offering: abbr.
25. Long, narrow inlet
26. "Julie & Julia" costar
27. Hesitation sounds

28. "Norma _____" (1979 Sally Field film)
29. Photocopier option: abbr.
31. Sue _____ Langdon
34. Temple tables
35. Without luster
37. The Mediterranean, e.g.
38. Make reference to

39. Like Death Valley
40. Singer Lovett
41. Name of 12 popes
42. Memo opening
43. "_____ in the Attic"
46. Ran into
47. U.N. host: abbr.

1	2	3	4	5		6	7	8		9	10	11
12						13				14		
15					16					17		
18				19				20	21			
			22				23					
24	25	26				27					28	29
30					31				32			
33				34				35				
		36					37					
38	39					40				41	42	43
44				45	46				47			
48				49				50				
51				52				53				

Answers on page 191.

SHIMMER AND SHINE

ACROSS

1. Be indebted to
4. Tight closure
8. Wistful phrase
12. Common rodent
13. Glamour rival
14. Sound of thunder
15. Wrist adornment
17. Kitchen utensils
18. Sound of wet impact
19. Color fabric, '60s-style
21. Cartoon Betty
24. Capture
25. Tops of aprons
28. Sting of pearls
32. Historic period
33. Heroic tales
34. At the present time
35. Hoops or studs
37. Advantage
38. Boring routine
39. Once around the sun
41. Adjusted beforehand
44. Scenic overlook
48. Solemn affirmation
49. Pinned jewelry
52. Dust _____
53. German automaker
54. Wallch or Whitney
55. Beseeched
56. Marsh grass stalk
57. Jolson or Gore

DOWN

1. Globes
2. Distort
3. Latin and "others": abbr.
4. Take care of
5. Building wing
6. Schooner filler
7. Latvian
8. Request another hearing
9. Hair-control accessory
10. Numerous
11. If all _____ fails…
16. Taxis
20. Pen fluids
22. "_____ even keel"
23. Lee or Bundy
25. Mayberry aunt
26. Tax-defered asset: abbr.
27. Hair clasp
29. Perry Mason story
30. Gear tooth
31. Female sheep
33. Location on the web
36. Hurried
37. Clapton or Carmen
40. Stay away from
41. Stately display
42. Train stack

43. Ski slope conveyance
45. Stadium replaced in 2009 by Citi Field
46. Kiss and _____

47. Buyer-beware warning
50. Regret
51. Praiseful poem

Answers on page 192.

DIET CONSCIOUS

ACROSS
1. Autobahn auto
4. Beer bottle top
7. Diet with an intake of certain liquids
12. Equinox month: abbr.
13. Flamenco yell
14. Knotted scarf
15. Add-on for Gator
16. Round object that can be eaten on a 55-Across diet
17. Perhaps
18. Big name in weight loss and diet programs
21. "Be there in just _____!"
22. Bug's antenna
26. Vietnam's capital
29. Nest egg inits.
30. Diet inspired by eating patterns around a European sea
35. "Let's call _____ night"
36. Doglike scavenger
37. Hollywood's Hedy
40. Song spelled with arm motions
43. Diet named for a Miami locale
47. Finds fault
50. Kia model
51. Wine and dine
52. Beaded counters of old
53. Wrap up
54. Bobble the ball, e.g.
55. Diet without animal consumption
56. Messy place
57. "CSI" evidence": abbr.

DOWN
1. Key of Brahms's Piano Trio No. 1 : abbr.
2. Movie matriarch played by Tyler Perry
3. Small songbirds
4. Imitator
5. One of the Baldwin brothers
6. Tree for a partridge in song
7. Oscar winner Foxx for "Ray"
8. Gas bill info
9. Wintry
10. Kernel holder
11. Summer on the Seine
19. Grape soda brand
20. Blazing
23. Commit perjury
24. Laundry brand
25. Bled in the wash
27. Jacket named for an Indian leader
28. Suffix of direct or transit

30. "Cool" amount at a heist
31. Greek H
32. River blocker
33. "Is _____ there?"
34. Christen
38. U.S. pet protector: abbr.
39. Violin bow application
41. Imitated a crow

42. Oak-to-be
44. "_____ bien!" : Fr.
45. Subtle help
46. Celebratory dance
47. Cleveland NBAer, for short
48. Bearded president, for short
49. Dust cloth

Answers on page 192.

BUY BUY BUY

ACROSS

1. Busy people in April: abbr.
5. Heat broadcasts: abbr.
9. Protrude
12. Bindle carrier
13. National park in Utah
14. She's often blamed for a famous breakup
15. Where Napoleon went in 1814
16. Church volunteer
18. Math class subject, maybe
20. Tool for a cold mountain climber
21. "Hunny" seeker
24. Money for the golden years: abbr.
27. Hammer's locale
28. Souped-up
29. & 31 Oscar nominee for "Hoosiers"
32. Weird Al parody of a Michael Jackson song
33. How long a wait might seem to last
34. Thesaurus item: abbr.
35. His game show is often seen with Pat's
36. Treat the turkey
38. Stops moving

43. Glade
45. It may break in the game "The Oregon Trail"
46. Amorphous lump
47. Math class subject, for short
48. Burn in the kitchen
49. Bad thing to be poked
50. With all one's marbles
51. SportsCenter network

DOWN

1. "Hell's Kitchen" competitor
2. Sport with chukkers
3. It's shortened, for short
4. "Me too!"
5. Flowery shrubs
6. One of Islam's five
7. Popular injection
8. Wrench in the gears
9. Department of Labor training program
10. Pizzeria chain
11. A child often leaves it out
17. Destroy, in a way
19. Nail the test
22. Tyrant's command
23. It may be leaned on in anger
24. Brainstorming session output
25. "Keep it ____"

26. Come before
28. TV character whose name is Spanish for "stupid"
30. Frost interviewee
31. Bank heist victim, maybe
33. Enter carefully
36. Quotable baseball catcher
37. Rub out

39. They often have dirt wiped on them
40. Alimony recipients, perhaps
41. Reaction to a bad pick-up line
42. Sea bird
43. Must 44-Down
44. Fork over

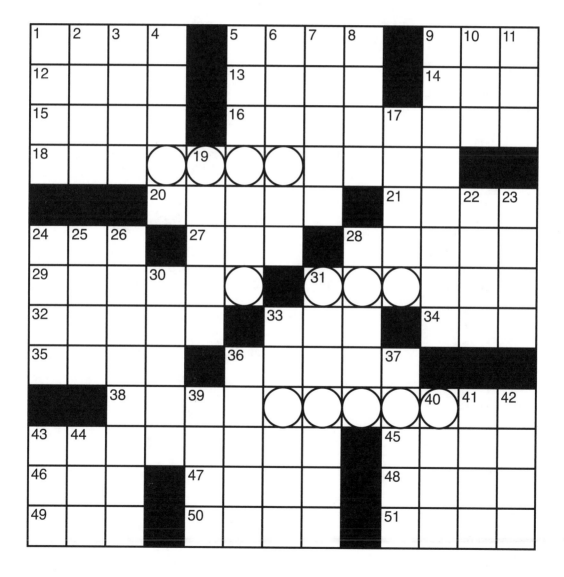

Answers on page 192.

ANSWERS

SONGS OF AMERICA (PAGE 4)

H	I	T	S		B	L	O	B		B	A	T
O	M	I	T		L	A	N	I		U	N	A
U	S	N	A		E	B	E	R		I	N	N
R	A	G	G	E	D	O	L	D	F	L	A	G
	D	E	N	S	E	R		B	A	D	L	Y
			A	S	L		J	A	L			
A	M	A	N	A		S	E	T	S	T	O	
P	A	R	T	Y	I	N	T	H	E	U	S	A
A	P	I		I	D	E	S		T	R	A	M
R	L	S		S	E	E	A		T	I	G	E
T	E	E		T	E	R	M		O	N	E	S

NURSERY RHYMES (PAGE 6)

F	I	N	A	L		T	A	P	A	S
A	D	A	M	E		A	L	A	M	O
R	O	S	E	S	A	R	E	R	E	D
		S	S	G	T		T	S	A	
S	P	R	S		R	N	A			
O	R	O		F	E	E	L	E	R	S
S	I	M	P	L	E	S	I	M	O	N
A	M	O	R	O	U	S		M	A	A
		Y	U	P		L	A	M	P	
C	E	E		R	O	T	O			
O	L	D	K	I	N	G	C	O	L	E
D	A	D	A	S		I	A	M	S	O
S	L	O	T	H		F	L	A	T	S

JANE AUSTEN (PAGE 8)

D	E	L	F	T		F	A	N	N	Y
C	L	A	R	A		R	E	L	E	E
C	A	P	E	K		O	C	A	L	A
		D	E	E	S		T	S	R	
E	N	C	E	I	N	T	E			
M	E	O	R		V	E	L	M	A	S
M	A	L	I	C		D	I	C	T	A
A	P	I	C	A	L		Z	A	N	Y
			K	R	A	K	A	T	O	A
U	N	A		R	O	W	B			
C	A	C	A	O		A	E	S	O	P
S	P	E	L	T		N	T	E	S	T
D	A	R	C	Y		S	H	E	A	S

EDGAR ALLAN POE (PAGE 10)

F	O	P	S		B	E	L	L	S
I	S	I	T	A		A	S	Y	L	A
T	H	E	B	L	A	C	K	C	A	T
O	E	R		B	I	T		E	M	I
F	A	R	R	A	R		H	E	A	R
	S	E	A	N	S		E	S	S	E
			V	O	C	A	L			
S	A	B	E		R	V	E	R	S	
C	H	A	N		E	O	N	I	A	N
O	C	T		P	E	I		P	T	A
T	H	E	P	E	N	D	U	L	U	M
C	O	A	C	T		S	H	E	R	E
H	O	U	S	E			S	Y	N	S

BAKER STREET REVISITED (PAGE 12)

S	L	A	B		T	H	E	M	E
H	E	L	L	S		B	R	A	V	E	D
A	V	I	A	N		A	I	L	I	N	G
W	I	T	H	O	U	T	A	C	L	U	E
			S	O	R	E	L	Y			
A	F	T		Z	E	D		O	V	E	R
I	R	E	N	E		A	N	I	T	A
M	Y	N	A		A	N	G		A	C	E
		M	O	R	A	L	S			
E	N	T	E	R	T	H	E	L	I	O	N
A	O	R	T	A	S		A	I	S	L	E
T	R	E	A	T	Y		M	E	L	D	S
S	I	E	G	E			R	E	S	T

UNUSUAL AMERICA (PAGE 14)

T	O	A	S	T	S		D	I	N	S
A	S	P	I	R	E		A	S	E	A
M	U	S	E	U	M	O	F	O	D	D
		G	L	I	N	T				
P	R	E	Y		T	E	D	S	
O	R	E	S		C	A	R	E	T	S
W	I	T		C	A	P		L	E	A
N	O	R	M	A	L		A	H	E	M
	R	O	A	D		T	R	I	P	
		G	E	A	R	S				
G	I	A	N	T	G	O	O	B	E	R
A	C	H	E		U	P	N	E	X	T
S	E	A	T		Y	E	S	S	E	S

ANSWERS

SUMMER CAMP (PAGE 16)

H	I	K	E	S		Z	U	L	U	S
C	H	O	S	E		I	R	I	N	A
A	N	D	O	R		P	E	R	I	S
		P	I	L	L		E	V	E	
I	V	E	H	A	D	I	T			
S	E	R	A		S	N	A	C	K	S
B	R	A	G	A		E	L	L	I	E
N	A	T	U	R	E		L	A	T	E
		S	C	R	E	A	M	E	D	
B	O	O		H	I	N	D			
O	R	A	T	E		I	E	V	E	R
R	E	F	E	R		A	G	E	N	A
N	O	S	E	Y		C	A	N	O	E

POTTERY (PAGE 22)

I	B	M	P	C		D	E	L	F	T
S	A	M	O	A		I	M	A	R	I
T	O	E	R	R		S	U	G	A	R
		C	O	R	R		S	T	E	
M	E	N	E	L	A	U	S			
A	N	I	L		U	P	T	I	C	K
I	D	T	A	G		T	O	M	E	I
N	O	S	I	E	R		N	A	T	L
			N	O	R	S	E	M	A	N
G	T	D		D	R	A	W			
J	H	U	R	U		G	A	N	G	S
A	U	R	I	C		O	R	D	E	R
C	R	O	C	K		S	E	A	T	O

SKYSCRAPERS (PAGE 18)

E	G	R	E	T		C	L	I	F	F
A	L	O	N	E		A	I	D	E	R
S	U	M	M	A		S	T	E	L	E
E	M	P	I	R	E	S	T	A	T	E
		T	Y	R	O	L				
B	O	N	Y		A	C	E	T	I	C
U	B	I		A	S	K		E	C	U
Y	I	P	P	E	E		M	E	E	T
		A	R	R	A	Y				
W	I	L	L	I	S	T	O	W	E	R
A	N	I	M	A		O	P	E	R	A
S	T	E	E	L		M	I	N	I	M
H	O	U	R	S		S	A	T	E	S

PALINDROMES (PAGE 24)

L	E	V	E	L		E	M	D	A	S	H
E	L	I	S	A		V	I	R	I	L	E
S	A	V	O	Y		E	N	A	M	O	R
S	T	E	P	O	N	N	O	P	E	T	S
		S	V	E	L	T	E				
H	E	D		E	R	Y		R	N	A	S
C	E	N	T	R		P	Y	L	O	N	
L	E	A	H		A	N	A		E	L	L
		U	P	R	O	S	E				
A	S	A	N	T	A	A	T	N	A	S	A
B	O	R	D	E	R		E	N	I	A	C
C	A	M	E	R	A		U	I	N	T	A
D	R	Y	R	O	T		R	O	T	O	R

SILENT LETTERS (PAGE 20)

S	C	A	M		D	E	B	T
P	A	U	L	O		M	I	N	E	O
A	S	T	I	N		I	N	T	E	R
R	T	E		R	E	C	E	I	P	T
E	L	U	S	I	V	E		C	E	E
		E	R	I	C	A		M	E	R
		M	E	D	E	A				
	S	A	P		E	M	M	A	S	
G	A	R		B	R	E	A	T	H	E
E	L	I	T	I	S	T		H	I	S
O	M	A	H	A		I	D	O	N	T
R	O	N	A	S		C	A	M	E	A
G	N	A	W			H	E	R	B	

HEIST MOVIES (PAGE 26)

H	E	A	T		R	E	A	R	E	D
E	L	C	I	D		A	M	R	I	T	A
S	A	M	M	I		N	A	N	O	O	K
T	H	E	B	A	N	K	J	O	B		
		A	L	I	I		S	A	H	L
I	T	A	L	I	A	N		M	E	A
R	U	M	E	N		E	S	B	A	T
A	B	U		T	O	P	K	A	P	I
S	A	S	S		A	T	O	Y		
		E	N	T	R	A	P	M	E	N	T
E	N	D	O	R	A		E	A	R	L	E
L	I	B	B	E	R		E	P	E	E	S
I	C	Y	S	E	A		S	I	R	S

ANSWERS

HASHTAG HUMOR (PAGE 28)

S	C	R	A	P		C	L	E	A	T
U	H	U	R	A		B	R	A	S	C	O
B	O	E	R	S		R	O	M	P	E	R
J	U	R	A	S	S	I	C	P	O	R	K
			Y	A	W	N	E	R	S	
P	E	A		G	E	E		E	I	N	E
E	R	A	S	E		M	Y	T	H	S
N	O	R	W		U	N	E		O	L	E
	D	E	A	L	S	T	O	
L	O	V	E	M	E	F	E	N	D	E	R
I	N	A	T	I	E		O	S	A	G	E
M	E	R	I	T	S		R	E	R	A	N
P	O	K	E	Y		S	T	A	D	T

WHODUNITS (PAGE 34)

T	E	A	R	S		A	L	T	A	R
E	C	L	A	T		A	N	O	I	N	T
T	H	E	M	O	O	N	S	T	O	N	E
E	O	S		L	O	N	E	R	
			S	E	O	U	L		A	P	U
M	A	L	O		A	M	S	T	E	L
T	H	E	H	O	L	L	O	W	M	A	N
G	O	S	O	L	O		A	S	K	A
E	Y	E		D	C	C	A	B	
			S	W	U	N	G		A	C	E
E	N	D	L	E	S	S	N	I	G	H	T
N	I	C	E	S	T		E	G	R	E	T
V	E	L	D	T		S	N	A	F	U

BOTANIC GARDENS (PAGE 30)

F	I	C	U	S		C	A	C	T	I
A	V	A	S	T		B	P	L	U	S
M	E	L	B	A		R	E	E	L	S
		O	R	C	A		O	E	O
L	A	S	T	R	A	D	A	
E	T	N	A		B	I	R	N	E	Y
A	K	I	N	S		O	B	E	S	E
F	A	T	I	M	A		O	R	A	L
		C	O	L	O	R	F	U	L
P	D	F		K	A	L	E	
A	I	O	L	I		A	T	O	N	E
I	N	N	I	E		F	U	S	E	S
L	O	T	U	S		S	M	A	R	T

THOREAU (PAGE 36)

C	I	V	I	L		W	A	L	D	E	N
A	N	I	M	E		O	N	E	I	D	A
S	M	O	O	T		R	A	G	O	U	T
S	E	L	F	R	E	L	I	A	N	C	E
			F	I	N	E	S	T	
E	T	A		D	A	Y		E	R	I	E
W	I	L	D	E		N	E	E	D	S
E	P	E	E		W	H	O		F	E	E
			C	A	R	E	T	S	
D	E	L	I	B	E	R	A	T	E	L	Y
E	X	O	D	U	S		S	O	B	E	R
N	I	C	E	S	T		T	R	A	I	L
S	T	A	S	E	S		E	E	N	S	Y

ARTS AND CRAFTS (PAGE 32)

G	L	U	E		P	A	P	E	R
P	I	L	A	R		A	U	R	O	R	A
A	T	A	R	I		R	E	E	L	I	N
S	A	N	D	P	A	I	N	T	I	N	G
		R	E	B	A	T	E	D	
O	N	E	O	N	O	N	E		E	S	D
C	O	R	P			O	N	T	V
S	H	A		A	S	S	O	R	T	E	D
	S	E	S	T	I	N	A	
B	E	A	D	N	E	C	K	L	A	C	E
A	M	B	I	E	N		E	L	E	M	S
F	E	L	L	A	S		Y	A	R	D	S
F	R	E	E	R		W	I	R	E

S.T.E.M. (PAGE 38)

F	I	E	L	D		T	O	M	E	S
R	O	D	E	O		W	R	O	T	E
E	N	G	I	N	E	E	R	I	N	G
E	S	E		E	X	E		L	A	O
			S	E	P	T	A	
S	I	T	U	S		S	C	R	I	M
C	L	A	M			T	E	C	H
I	L	I	A	C		V	I	D	E	O
		C	O	H	E	N	
O	K	S		M	E	L		T	O	E
M	A	T	H	E	M	A	T	I	C	S
E	L	I	O	T		R	E	C	A	P
N	E	R	D	S		S	A	S	S	Y

ANSWERS

SEEN AT THE GROCERY (PAGE 40)

Across/grid answers:
DUCK, HONEY, IKEA, WERENT, FRENCHBREAD, SUERS, BAABAA, TIP, ROSS, TISANE, PLASTICWRAP, MAITRE, AONE, SSR, ASANTE, LIBEL, TOMATOSAUCE, REDSOX, KNAR, LOSER, EATS

DIME STORES (PAGE 46)

FERNS, OHARE, IRATE, LALAW, FIVEANDDIME, ENISLE, DISS, TYCHO, ABE, TICTAC, BENFRANKLIN, CAVIAR, CDN, AMIGA, ATTN, NEWERA, CHICKENFEED, REMET, TURNA, EASES, SLOTH

SEEN AT PICNICS (PAGE 42)

FLASK, SCARE, ADLAI, HHOUR, DRINKCOOLER, EST, IAGO, CDLI, DAL, BRUNEI, DIRE, BARBECUEPIT, LINC, OTELLO, SDS, ACES, BRAN, DSM, INSECTSPRAY, MERLE, IRONS, SCALD, LOPAT

CONDIMENTS (PAGE 48)

SPAM, MAYAS, FLAK, BEGONE, OYSTERSAUCE, GLOSSIER, ACS, ONI, SOLE, XANADU, CHIMICHURRI, IOMOTH, MANE, SEA, MOS, ANATHEMA, HORSERADISH, ERRORS, ECHO, MASSE, NEED

LITTLE PESTS (PAGE 44)

CROP, ASIDE, HENRI, NUDES, ADMONITIONS, DAEMON, LYE, INTEL, OBAN, REINED, DUNEBUGGIES, AGENAS, ATOM, TAINT, BOA, OEUVRE, ENCHANTRESS, ACRID, SERVO, DEEDS, SAPS

CHARLES DICKENS (PAGE 50)

FAGIN, IDLING, AMICO, ROADEO, TILER, ALDINE, ARTFULDODGER, ANGERS, BOWL, ASE, TEA, OEILS, STARS, ZOE, KBS, HEEP, SILAGE, LITTLEDORRIT, ANGOLA, REECE, OLIVER, SILAS, SAFETY, ENOLS

ANSWERS

AESOP'S FABLES (PAGE 52)

Across/grid answers:
CAMEL · MOO · APE
ACELA · OCA · LEA
BELLINGTHECAT
SNEE · UGH
OPT · IANS · GENE
FARMER · KISMET
TRIO · STIR · YEA
SIR · EPIC
THELIONSSHARE
EEC · AWE · EIDER
ANT · LET · SPADE

PROGRAMMING LANGUAGES (PAGE 58)

PLEB · GENIE
LIRR · PINBOY
UMNO · SLOANE
SNOWBALL
SALSADIP
ANSELM · OCR
CHARM · LIMBO
ERR · TOTEMS
DAGUERRE
SQUIRREL
SADHUS · AERO
UPBEAT · TAMA
PEARL · ELAN

ROBERT B. PARKER BOOKS (PAGE 54)

STENO · BOAST
TACOS · EDGAR
DOUBLEDEUCE
LOGE · EKE
ACHE · OWL
CHI · SMILING
NIGHTANDDAY
ECHOING · LIP
ELI · GELS
ION · LATH
SPARECHANGE
LAMES · ENEMY
ELECT · MATTE

PARADES (PAGE 60)

MOMS · EASTER
EXAM · ABHORS
SERA · SIRENS
ANDRETTI
IMO · OLMEC
OBGYN · FLOAT
NOR · TSR
BRAUN · PLOYS
YESNO · AAR
KITTYCAT
RAPIDO · MAXI
EARNER · EDEN
MAYDAY · NEST

RIDERS IN THE SKY (PAGE 56)

DEERE · ALERT
ARRAY · SINEW
WINGEDHORSE
SCOLDS · NICE
AROW · CUT
CHINO · ACHES
RAM · PERL
IRAS · AGENDA
SAGITTARIUS
IRENE · MIRES
SEDGE · ECOLE

NEOLOGISMS (PAGE 62)

FLAG · CRUETS
LADE · LESSEE
ATOM · IPECAC
PER · AFAR
KEPIS · MAE
SHADE · TEALS
AABA · SNAP
SALMI · MASSY
SSE · SYRUP
BROS · LUG
BATEAU · EASE
SANSEI · KIEL
CATTLE · ENDS

MYSTERY WRITERS (PAGE 64)

```
D R U P E   N A O M I
R I G I D   U S H E R
J O H N G R I S H A M
    T E A S   I S A
D E W S   C A N
O V A   C O N C A V E
H A R L A N C O B E N
A N N E T T E   L T D
    T A E   S E S S
E P A   L U L L
K A T H Y R E I C H S
G U R U S   A D I O S
S L A N T   H E D G E
```

BLUEGRASS (PAGE 70)

```
A L A S   B A T   B O T H
D O V E   U N A   O B O E
D U E L I N G B A N J O S
S I R E N   S O N N E T S
  E T C H   T O T   T H E
    T U N   S O D
A L E   M A L   N O E S
T O N N A G E   Y A L T A
R O V I N G G A M B L E R
I K O N   E G G   L E A K
A S I A   R Y E   E N D S
```

LARGE NUMBERS (PAGE 66)

```
M E N D S   S H O R T A
A C E I T   A E I O U Y
D U O D E C I L L I O N
D A N S E U S E S
    T P S   N E V I S
W A R   L A B   A A R E
T R E D E C I L L I O N
W A D E   K O A   O C S
O M A R R   N P R
    B A L D E A G L E
V I G I N T I L L I O N
E N N E A D   E L A N D
R O U S T S   D Y N E S
```

BARBERSHOP QUARTET SONGS (PAGE 72)

```
A B B E S S   T A S K S
L A R V A E   H I R E S
S W E E T A D E L I N E
O L D   I M A M S
    S N A R E   D A B
D E N I E R   S O D O
I D O N T K N O W W H Y
A D D S   U B E N D S
L Y E   P A R S E
    D E D E E   B R O
U P A L A Z Y R I V E R
S E E I T   E V A D N E
P E R I S   V E S S E L
```

FLIGHT CREW (PAGE 68)

```
R O B I N   E G R E T
E A R T O   S U E M E
S H I E S   I M M I E
H U M M I N G B I R D
    I R O N O N
A M A Z E S   D R E
W I L E E   S K E E T
L A P   S P I R E D
    H E G O A T
S P A R R O W H A W K
A U D R A   N A V A L
S M O O T   E R I K A
E A G L E   R A V E N
```

WEIGHTS & MEASURES (PAGE 74)

```
S T O N E   S L U R   R E A M
P I N O T   E A S E   O N T O
I R I S H   A Y E S   A T O P
N E T H E R M O S T   D I N E
    R E E F   S P I C E D
A I R S   I N F O   H E E D S
L O W I N G   S O F A
F U R L O N G   H A S T E N S
    I S I S   T E R R O R
P L O T S   N A S H   Y E T I
B A R R E L   I T O N
A S I A   I L L U M I N A T E
N S E C   M A I D   G E N O A
D I N K   O M N I   H A D E S
J E T S   S A G O   T R Y S T
```

ANSWERS

U.S. CITIES
(PAGE 76)

```
ATLAS  ERLE  HANA
IRATE  MEET  ODES
NEWORLEANS  NOCK
TENN  ERIN  DOLCE
   CANARYYELLOW
GONERIL  SABU
RTE  ENDS  STLUKE
ATOP  SIC  UTES
BOSTON  DALE  APT
   OBEY  MEMPHIS
PHILADELPHIA
RAVEN  SOFA  SACK
ADAM  ASPIRATION
DENY  PEER  RONEE
ASTI  ESSE  CRUDE
```

O CANADA
(PAGE 82)

```
SEAM  CSPAN  SNEE
SUMO  RETRO  KERN
GRIT  IWANTMYMTV
TORONTO  HALOES
   REIN  BALI
QUEBEC  MANITOBA
ASOUR  MINK  ROT
TELS  LANES  DOVE
ANI  EYES  RONIN
ROCKSTAR  KOMODO
   APES  NEHI
BEAVER  OPENBAR
DINNERBELL  IONE
ANTE  IRATE  ORTS
YEAR  PARER  NEST
```

THE BODY HUMAN
(PAGE 78)

```
GAGA  TIAMO  RUM
ALAN  HANGIN  ACE
LIMN  ELAINE  DOT
 SMALLINTESTINE
   ALEE  ARCSIN
BRR  ONES  AOK
REAP  EPIGLOTTIS
IDYLL  ASA  PSHAW
MOSAIC  TIM  KANE
  NEATENUP  TSE
 CLEANER  SIPS
FEEDBIN  TCELLS
ADD  ENAMEL  AILS
MAG  DENOTE  CFOS
ERE  SSTAR  EEGS
```

AMERICAN IDOL
(PAGE 84)

```
REAP  HIP  MUDS
ELLA  OWE  ENYA
CLARKSON  ADES
   TIE  STRESS
RADON  EAR
EVEN  AIDA  WAR
DIG  ABDUL  ONE
ODE  MEAN  TONE
  NEE  PEDAL
STERNO  CON
HORA  STUDDARD
IDES  SIR  ELIA
POSE  OLD  RIND
```

TELEVISION
(PAGE 80)

```
MAIDS  SWAG  OONA
ADIEU  AARP  FLAM
REIGN  THEOFFICE
SSI  REEL  ODORS
   HITE  PHRASES
GREYSANATOMY
NUTMEG  SUMS  TDS
ASON  ERNIE  LIRA
TEN  ERIE  LSEVEN
 ICECREAMSODA
OMIGOSH  UNOS
DONEN  ORDO  TMZ
DOCTORWHO  TAHOE
ESAI  CROP  HAUTE
REST  ASHE  SAGES
```

FAMOUS AMERICANS
(PAGE 86)

```
MASSE  LASSO  SDS
OSAKA  ODEAR  ART
COLINPOWELL  LOI
SNOW  IRAE  DOWN
  NEILARMSTRONG
   ACC  TEENSY
HARRYHOUDINI
ELA  TRULY
ABNERDOUBLEDAY
PARSES  AEDES
  AMELIAEARHART
ANGEL  ALAW  OGEE
LOG  ELMORE  RIVA
ERE  REBELS  NOAM
CAD  SASSY  SSNS
```

COOKING "P"S (PAGE 88)

```
L O G S   C A U L K   R A S A
A L I T   R U P E E   E M I L
M E R E   A R S O N   S A G O
P O L E N T A     P E N N E
      P E E L   N E H R U
S C A L E D   P O P O V E R
W A D E D   S E R E   E N I D
A G O   S C H E M E S   S L Y
G E L S   R I P S   A L I K E
D E E P E N S   I B I S E S
    S T O W S   S T E M
C A C T I     P A R B O I L
O G E E   E T H Y L   E L S E
C A N E   M A O R I   R I B S
A R T S   S O N I C   S O N S
```

BEST PICTURE OSCAR WINNERS (PAGE 94)

```
R A M P   P U N T   N A D A
E A R L   A M O K   D O P E Y
T H E A R T I S T   A N O L E
      N O O N E   A D E
A B S T A I N   P L A T O O N
P R E E N S   A L I I   C N S
T E R R   A R I A S   A E C
  W E S T S I D E S T O R Y
S S N   H A D E S   C I E L
I K E   I R A N   S H A N A S
B I R D M A N   C L I P A R T
      I B N   S H I F T
C A N A L   G L A D I A T O R
A D E L E   R O S E   I R O N
D O T S   S E E S   N A P A
```

THE VIEW (PAGE 90)

```
S P F   A C E   B A S
T E E   B U D   E W E
G O L D B E R G   H A T H
A L L   E L L E   A R T E
G E E S E     A R D E N
A N T E   S U R I   S R S
      W A L T E R S
O M S   G O A D   P I P E
B A N J O     C A M E L
O R E O   R E P O   P E A
E G A N   O D O N N E L L
I K E   T I S   O D E
E S S   S T Y   W E D
```

ANIMAL WORDS (PAGE 96)

```
S T A G   C O L D S   C R O P
O H I O   A L O E S   H U L A
L A R D   B I B L E   I B I S
D I S S O L V E   S A B O T
      E P E E   O P I N E
S L A N T S   B E R T R A M
T I L D E   A B E R   I N F O
R A P   D A M A S K S   E O N
O N E S   B I T E   L U C R E
P A N T I E S   M O N K E Y
    H E F T S   L A S S
S T O P S   E I G H T I E S
C A R P   V I X E N   R O V E
O R N E   I M A G E   A W E S
T E S S   C O M E T   P A S S
```

BROADWAY MUSICALS BY SONGS (PAGE 92)

```
L Y R I C   I B I S   H A H A
L E O N A   N O O K   O M E N
B A N A L   T O N I   S E I N
S R S   T H E K I N G A N D I
    P E O R I A   U N T I E
H I B A C H I   N A A N
O K L A H O M A   S M A R T S
L E A R     G P S   O R E
D A B   S A B R A   C U T I E
    M E N E   L A M P O O N
G U Y S A N D D O L L S
L S A T S   R E O S   C A S E
O O L A   R O C K O F A G E S
O N E R   D O R A   A L A R M
M E S S   A M Y S   T E R S E
```

10-LETTER WORDS (PAGE 98)

```
P A N E   A L A I   H M O S
A B O M I N A B L E   M A N Y
D E L E C T A B L E   S S T S
D A R E I   R T E S   Q A T
    I M S O   R E A D U P
T A B L E   A N Y   R U E
O R L   N A T O   R A M R O D
U N A S   C Y B E R S P A C E
R O C K N E   L D S   S D A K
K I A   B Y O   U S E S A
A S P I R E   M Y S T
B U M   R O M P   A H O O T
A D I N   W O O D P E C K E R
S I T E   E A R M A R K I N G
S O H O   N E A T   S E N T
```

ANSWERS

WORLD HISTORY (PAGE 100)

Crossword solution grid:
- HARM · PEPUP · LADS
- AMOK · ROUSH · AREA
- WALTDISNEY · OPED
- SHOGUN · YESITSME
- ELS · CCS · IMS
- THECONQUEROR
- SATAY · LAIUS · ERO
- USED · TERSE · AFTS
- BEE · SIREE · SWISS
- JAMESMADISON
- STB · STD · ASP
- TREASURE · MOOSHU
- HILL · KUBLAIKHAN
- ELSE · TIBER · LOKI
- ELAN · UNSAY · AWAC

SCIENCE (PAGE 106)

Crossword solution grid:
- EATS · SHEAF · SITS
- MIRA · TOOLE · ARIA
- IDOL · IONIZATION
- TEDTALKS · HESSE
- IGLU · TAOS
- GYMNOSPERMS · PAT
- OARED · NEAT · RUE
- OHMS · CONES · CAGE
- FOO · ACLU · AUDEN
- YOM · SEDIMENTARY
- SODS · OMNI
- WATER · LOBOTOMY
- APPLESAUCE · OGEE
- ISEE · ASTOR · ULAN
- FEDS · WHEWS · TENS

WEIRD NATURE (PAGE 102)

Crossword solution grid:
- EBAN · RAINS · ACAP
- RARA · ERNIE · LOTI
- ANTARCTICA · ERIC
- DECODE · ETS · ONA
- LAMPS · DRAWINGS
- ANI · ECHO · CAMELS
- BASS · COLL · MATEO
- WAXPOETIC
- ABDEL · ERGO · SAME
- SLEEPS · ESTD · BAR
- FEATHERS · EERIE
- ASL · ANU · POLLEN
- RSTU · OPENSESAME
- AMIS · RENOS · ISAT
- SENS · SEEME · ETNA

RIVERS (PAGE 108)

Crossword solution grid:
- SPAS · MOWAT · SWIM
- LILT · IWISH · OHNO
- OPERASERIA · BIDS
- BESETS · EMMA · TUE
- AEONS · EXCESS
- ASKOUT · ASIAN
- PO · FREER · SLOPE
- HAFT · ISLES · LIAM
- ELTON · TITLE · STS
- BOOMS · HUSHES
- AMONRA · MAGNA
- GAI · MIME · FEINTS
- NILE · TASTESGOOD
- ENER · ANAIS · HITA
- WEDS · INSET · TREK

SHAKESPEARE (PAGE 104)

Crossword solution grid:
- ARGON · ROME · FDR
- TARSI · ELIA · SANE
- THETEMPEST · PLAT
- IRE · CEE · CARESTO
- LANTERN · BETTER
- AHSO · ITSELF · AST
- MAT · CLEO · FTS
- EKED · SEA · REFS
- ALI · ECON · AMA
- SSN · XANADU · SECT
- SIGNET · OTHELLO
- UNLACES · MOE · LET
- MOET · REDASABEET
- ERAS · ETUI · TERSE
- SER · RIEN · SLYER

PAINTERS (PAGE 110)

Crossword solution grid:
- SEAS · CALF · TAPAS
- ALIT · ARIA · INAPT
- LADA · NEON · PCLAB
- AMERICANGOTHIC
- SVU · NOONE
- INDIANAPACER
- DEIGN · BADE · OIL
- LEONARDODAVINCI
- EDS · OULU · ONEUP
- PABLOPICASSO
- EMILE · RAS
- JACKSONPOLLOCK
- PERKY · ROAN · UPON
- ICALL · BARE · MAHI
- ETTES · SHED · PLOT

ANSWERS

MYTHOLOGY (PAGE 112)

B	O	N	E	S		S	C	A	N		S	P	A	N
A	L	O	N	E		C	H	O	O		T	I	D	E
R	A	G	G	E	D	Y	A	N	N		R	E	Z	A
S	Y	S		M	E	L	T		S	P	I	D	E	R
			R	E	E	L		I	T	I	N	A		
A	G	F	A		P	A	D	D	I	N	G	T	O	N
L	O	O	M	S			R	I	C	E		E	M	O
C	L	U		P	A	L	O	O	K	A		R	E	B
O	E	R		A	B	U	M			L	A	R	G	E
A	M	B	E	R	A	L	E	R	T		R	E	A	L
	A	M	E	N	U			H	O	S	T			
A	S	G	A	R	D		T	I	N	T		H	E	M
M	A	G	I		O	R	A	N	G	E	S	O	D	A
O	N	E	L		N	E	R	O		T	O	L	E	T
S	E	R	S		S	A	P	S		S	W	A	N	S

MUSIC (PAGE 114)

Z	E	N	D	A		A	R	E	S		I	N	T	S
A	L	O	E	S		S	A	G	A		N	E	U	N
C	A	R	L	Y	S	I	M	O	N		T	A	P	A
	M	O	L	E	S			T	A	U	T	E	R	
A	T	A	R	U	N		P	H	A	R	R	E	L	L
R	O	R	E	M		A	A	U		A	N	N	O	Y
N	C	A	A		O	S	T	L	E	R				
	K	E	N	D	R	I	C	K	L	A	M	A	R	
			B	L	A	H		S	T	E	N	O	S	
F	L	O	R	A		G	U	S		N	A	T	O	
J	A	N	I	S	J	O	P	L	I	N		G	O	B
O	N	S	P	E	C		I	N	O	U	R			
R	A	T	E		R	E	C	E	N	T	P	A	S	T
D	I	A	N		E	N	D	S		T	O	M	M	Y
S	S	R	S		W	E	S	T		E	N	S	U	E

ROBERTS RULES (PAGE 116)

M	I	L	L		B	R	O	S		E	A	T
A	S	E	A		L	E	A	P		A	R	R
S	A	N	C	T	U	A	R	Y		G	E	E
T	W	O	T	O	E	D		R	E	L	A	Y
			O	R	A		R	I	D	E		
M	A	C		I	N	G	E		N	E	R	O
M	I	D	N	I	G	H	T	B	A	Y	O	U
E	X	P	O		E	I	R	E		E	N	T
		L	U	L	L		A	L	P			
I	R	A	N	I		T	I	L	A	P	I	A
T	A	Y		B	O	R	N	I	N	I	C	E
E	V	E		R	O	U	E		D	E	A	R
M	I	R		A	P	E	D		A	T	N	O

FANCY PARTY ATTIRE (PAGE 118)

U	P	A		J	U	T		B	L	A	C	K
M	A	L		A	N	Y		O	U	T	R	E
B	T	U		M	I	R		O	C	E	A	N
R	I	M		S	T	O	C	K	I	N	G	S
A	N	N	E				R	I	A			
	A	A	S		P	O	I	S				
S	E	Q	U	I	N	S	H	A	W	L		
			R	E	A	P		Y	E	A		
		C	C	C				E	L	B	E	
H	I	G	H	H	E	E	L	S		F	E	R
A	T	A	R	I		N	O	T		A	L	I
R	E	P	I	N		D	R	Y		R	E	C
D	R	E	S	S		S	E	X		E	R	A

ANCHORWOMEN (PAGE 120)

H	O	L	E		I	N	G	E		L	E	D
I	R	A	Q		N	A	R	C		A	P	E
M	E	N	U		O	V	A	L		Z	E	E
	D	I	A	N	E	S	A	W	Y	E	R	
		N	N	E		P	I	E				
J	A	D	E	D		B	A	R	B	A	R	A
A	T	E		T	U	T		R	E	P		
W	A	L	T	E	R	S		P	Q	R	S	T
	A	L	A		T	A	U					
K	A	T	I	E	C	O	U	R	I	C		
O	F	A		C	H	A	R		N	O	E	L
F	A	N		T	E	R	N		C	A	K	E
I	R	K		S	A	S	S		E	X	E	S

JUST SHOE ME (PAGE 122)

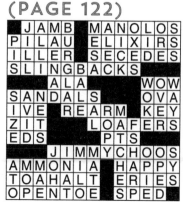

	J	A	M	B		M	A	N	O	L	O	S
P	I	L	A	U		E	L	I	X	I	R	S
I	L	L	E	R		S	E	C	E	D	E	S
S	L	I	N	G	B	A	C	K	S			
			A	L	A				W	O	W	
S	A	N	D	A	L	S		O	V	A		
I	V	E		R	E	A	R	M		K	E	Y
Z	I	T			L	O	A	F	E	R	S	
E	D	S				P	T	S				
	J	I	M	M	Y	C	H	O	O	S		
A	M	M	O	N	I	A		H	A	P	P	Y
T	O	A	H	A	L	T		E	R	I	E	S
O	P	E	N	T	O	E		S	P	E	D	

FUNNY FEMALES
(PAGE 124)

O	R	A	L		B	O	Z		S	L	E	D
L	O	B	E		A	D	E	L	A	I	D	E
L	A	R	A	I	N	E	N	E	W	M	A	N
A	D	O	R	N	S			A	D	A	M	S
		G	N	U		E	C	R	U			
I	R	A		R	O	V	E		S	H	A	G
C	A	T	H	E	R	I	N	E	T	A	T	E
E	P	E	E		A	C	T	S		B	E	E
		A	U	N	T		S	P	A			
A	B	E	T	S			S	E	A	N	C	E
R	O	S	I	E	O	D	O	N	N	E	L	L
T	R	A	N	S	F	E	R		E	R	A	S
S	N	U	G		F	E	E		L	A	N	E

MELTS IN YOUR MOUTH
(PAGE 126)

A	W	L		P	E	E	P		E	G	A	D
L	I	E		A	M	M	O		D	E	V	O
I	N	B		P	I	P	I	N	G	H	O	T
	E	L	M	I	R	A		E	E	R	I	E
E	B	A	Y		T	W	A		Y	D	S	
V	A	N	N	A	W	H	I	T	E			
A	R	C	A	D	E		L	L	A	M	A	S
			H	A	R	V	E	Y	M	I	L	K
M	A	S		G	E	O		E	L	L	A	
A	S	C	I	I		Y	E	S	S	I	R	
C	H	O	C	O	L	A	T	E		E	I	N
H	E	R	E		A	G	O	G		U	S	E
O	N	E	S		X	E	N	A		S	E	W

GENE KELLY
(PAGE 128)

P	A	D			D	N	A		P	E	A	R
O	B	I		L	A	O	S		A	R	L	O
L	E	S		A	N	T	I		R	O	A	D
		C	Y	D	C	H	A	R	I	S	S	E
S	P	O	U	S	E		T	I	S			
A	L	U	M		S	I	C		I	C	E	
D	O	N	A	L	D	O	C	O	N	N	O	R
A	P	T		A	O	L		E	A	R	L	
		M	I	N		B	R	O	N	T	E	
J	U	D	Y	G	A	R	L	A	N	D		
A	R	U	G		H	E	A	P		O	U	R
I	D	E	A		U	N	I	T		U	S	A
L	U	L	L		E	E	R		T	E	M	

THE DRESS
(PAGE 130)

G	E	L		F	L	E	A		S	L	A	P
A	M	A		R	E	A	P		L	A	M	E
N	I	K		A	A	R	P		A	T	O	Z
G	R	E	E	N	S	L	E	E	V	E	S	
		E	L	K		A	X	E				
O	K	R	A		U	S	E		P	A	D	
V	E	I	L	O	F	S	E	C	R	E	C	Y
A	Y	E		S	L	O		O	N	C	E	
		S	H	E		E	A	T				
	R	U	N	A	W	A	Y	T	R	A	I	N
J	O	S	E		O	X	E	N		G	N	U
A	L	D	A		U	L	N	A		O	D	D
B	E	A	K		T	E	S	S		N	Y	E

TRIPLE CROWN
(PAGE 132)

R	E	A	M		B	R	A		L	O	U	
E	A	S	E		A	I	L	S		O	N	S
F	R	A	N	K	R	O	B	I	N	S	O	N
	S	P	U	N		T	A	R	O			
			I	R	E		S	L	A	V	E	
A	H	A		F	A	R			A	R	I	D
M	I	C	K	E	Y		M	A	N	T	L	E
E	R	I	N		B	E	L		S	A	N	
S	E	D	A	N		A	N	T				
		V	O	I	T		A	S	I	A		
R	O	G	E	R	S	H	O	R	N	S	B	Y
A	N	A		M	E	E	K		O	L	L	A
T	E	D			E	D	S		W	E	E	K

PRETTY WOMAN
(PAGE 134)

L	O	S		S	M	E	E		I	T	E	M
A	N	T		T	A	R	A		D	A	L	I
M	A	E		E	R	A	S		I	S	L	E
	P	R	E	T	T	Y	W	O	M	A	N	
		A	L	I			E	T	A			
A	G	A	R		N	U	M	B		N	O	W
M	O	N	A	L	I	S	A	S	M	I	L	E
C	O	G		I	S	N	T		E	A	D	S
	S	A	L			A	V	A				
N	O	T	T	I	N	G	H	I	L	L		
O	K	R	A		C	A	A	N		O	D	D
D	I	O	R		O	G	R	E		V	I	A
S	E	M	I		S	A	I	D		E	G	G

ANSWERS

FASHION FORWARD
(PAGE 136)

O	W	L	S		A	B	E	S		V	E	T
R	I	O	T		D	U	D	E		E	W	E
C	L	A	I	B	O	R	N	E		R	E	X
A	D	D	L	E		E	A	R	H	A	R	T
			E	L	B	A		S	A	W		
N	A	G		T	O	U	R		Z	A	P	S
F	L	I	M	S	Y		H	A	Y	N	I	E
L	I	V	E		S	U	E	D		G	E	T
		E	A	R		N	A	I	L			
P	O	N	T	I	A	C		E	A	S	E	S
I	N	C		S	T	L	A	U	R	E	N	T
N	T	H		K	R	O	C		G	A	Z	A
S	O	Y		S	A	G	E		E	T	O	N

PATRIOTIC CLOTHES
(PAGE 142)

T	E	E	N	A	G	E	R		S	C	O	T
E	L	D	O	R	A	D	O		H	O	B	O
R	E	D	R	I	D	I	N	G	H	O	O	D
M	C	I			S	T	A	Y		K	I	A
S	T	E	L	E			M	O	I	S	T	
			A	L	E	R	T		F	E	T	E
	W	H	I	T	E	H	A	T	S			
C	O	A	T		S	T	Y	L	E			
A	R	R	I	D			I	N	L	A	Y	
S	E	M		R	A	T	A		E	R	E	
B	L	U	E	S	T	O	C	K	I	N	G	S
A	S	P	S		I	N	M	O	T	I	O	N
H	E	S	S		T	I	E	S	I	N	T	O

HAIL MARY
(PAGE 138)

O	B	A	M	A		O	F	F		A	R	F
T	Y	L	E	R		F	I	R		H	E	R
S	E	I	N	E		A	L	E		I	N	A
			D	N	A		L	E	A	K	E	Y
C	A	S	S	A	T	T		B	R	E	W	S
U	M	P			A	W	A	I	T			
B	A	Y		B	L	I	G	E		J	O	G
			G	E	E	S	E		O	U	I	
E	E	R	I	E		T	R	A	V	E	R	S
S	T	U	A	R	T		S	R	A			
S	U	N		G	U	M		O	L	D	E	N
A	D	O		U	S	A		M	O	O	R	E
Y	E	N		T	H	Y		A	R	N	A	Z

LITTLE WOMEN
(PAGE 144)

P	A	T		W	A	G	E		P	L	A	Y
I	R	A		A	R	E	A		L	O	R	E
T	A	X	SHE	L	T	E	R		A	S	K	S
T	B	I	R	D		L	A	Z	E			
			R	O	A	R		C	A	SHE	W	S
S	L	A	Y		T	A	T	E		A	H	A
A	O	L		F	I	SHE	R	S		R	E	F
A	L	L		O	P	R	Y		E	T	T	E
B	A	Y	O	U		S	A	W	S			
		SHE	A	R	S		A	P	A	R	T	
O	D	E	S		H	E	R	SHE	Y	B	A	R
A	U	D	I		U	S	E	R		B	I	O
K	E	Y	S		E	P	P	S		A	N	T

GIRL, BY ANOTHER NAME
(PAGE 140)

P	C	B		Z	I	T	I		G	A	S	P
A	O	L		E	M	I	L		O	L	E	O
I	L	E		B	A	L	K		S	E	E	P
L	O	W	E	R	C	L	A	S	S			
	R	A	T	A				T	I	M	E	I
S	A	F	E		L	A	T	E	P	A	S	S
E	D	U		H	A	B	I	T		C	P	L
L	A	S	V	E	G	A	S		F	A	R	E
A	N	E	A	R			S	U	R	E		
		L	A	T	I	N	C	R	O	S	S	
E	S	A	I		O	D	E	R		O	S	U
L	U	L	U		N	O	R	A		N	O	D
F	I	L	M		G	L	O	P		S	S	S

THE IT BAG
(PAGE 146)

K	N	O	T		L	A	S		P	T	A	S
E	R	I	E		O	F	T		R	A	R	A
G	A	L	A		F	R	I		A	L	A	S
			M	O	T	O	R	C	Y	C	L	E
S	P	E	E	D	Y		F	O	E			
E	L	U	D	E		A	R	T	D	E	C	O
T	O	R		S	P	Y		W	O	K		
S	T	O	P	G	A	P		B	L	A	I	R
			E	A	U		S	I	E	N	N	A
P	A	D	D	I	N	G	T	O	N			
L	I	R	A		T	O	O		T	R	O	Y
O	D	I	N		E	G	O		I	O	W	A
D	E	B	T		R	I	P		L	I	L	Y

ANSWERS

CUBIC ZIRCONIA (PAGE 148)

```
L I T H E ■ T L C ■ A S K
P O B O X ■ O O O ■ Q U I
G U S T O ■ M A R Q U I S
A S P ■ T U B ■ E T A T S
■ ■ ■ T I S ■ E R R ■ ■ ■
P R I N C E S S ■ ■ J O Y
J I L T ■ D E C ■ O A H U
S O L ■ ■ T E A R D R O P
■ ■ ■ S F O ■ P O D ■ ■ ■
J E L L O ■ D E B ■ A R K
E M E R A L D ■ B E L I E
E M S ■ M E A ■ E M P T Y
R Y E ■ Y A Y ■ R U S E S
```

VIDEO FAVES (PAGE 154)

```
S C A B ■ G A S ■ C P A S
S L U R ■ I D A ■ R E M O
W A D E ■ N I B ■ E N O L
■ W I N O N A R Y D E R ■
■ ■ ■ N A Y ■ I D O L ■ ■
A S T A R ■ R N S ■ O R R
J O H N ■ R I A ■ M P A A
A X E ■ R E D ■ S U E D E
■ ■ B E E B ■ S T L ■ ■ ■
■ V I N C E V A U G H N ■
B A R N ■ C O N ■ R E A D
A N D I ■ C O D ■ E R I S
T E S S ■ A M Y ■ W A L T
```

CELEBS WITH TWINS (PAGE 150)

```
D A N K ■ E B B S ■ R F D
I R A N ■ T O U T ■ A I R
R E B E C C A R O M I J N
T A S E R ■ C B R A D I O
■ ■ ■ L A W ■ S E C ■ ■ ■
M U M ■ W I G ■ ■ H I V E
A N G E L I N A J O L I E
C O M A ■ ■ U N E ■ L E E
■ ■ ■ T O R ■ T W A ■ ■ ■
A R S E N I C ■ E M C E E
J E N N I F E R L O P E Z
A B A ■ O L D E ■ C A L I
R A G ■ N E E D ■ O S S O
```

COUNTRY FOLK (PAGE 156)

```
C L A P ■ I L K ■ E D N A
C A L L ■ G A I ■ D O E S
R I P A ■ L I S ■ W R A P
■ T A Y L O R S W I F T ■
■ ■ ■ C I A O ■ E O N ■ ■
S M I T H S ■ D W A Y N E
I A N ■ ■ ■ ■ ■ ■ A I L
S H O W E R ■ C O U N T Y
■ ■ ■ I L O ■ H A N K ■ ■
■ D O L L Y P A R T O N ■
H E A L ■ A L I ■ I V A N
M A H I ■ L O S ■ E I N E
O N U S ■ E Y E ■ S C A T
```

APPLIANCE ATTACHMENTS (PAGE 152)

```
S W I G ■ R U E ■ P E A S
A R N O ■ A N T H I L L S
W A F F L E I R O N M A N
S P R E E ■ ■ E B B ■ ■ ■
■ ■ O R G A N ■ O A S I S
S I N ■ A T O P ■ L E N A
H O T P L A T E G L A S S
O N O R ■ N E R O ■ T O E
D A F O E ■ S U M A C ■ ■
■ ■ ■ G R E ■ ■ E L O P E
G A S R A N G E R O V E R
N O T A S O U L ■ H E L M
P L U M ■ S N L ■ A R E A
```

ON THE SCREEN (PAGE 158)

```
A N T S ■ G O D ■ A J A R
S C A T ■ A V A ■ S O L O
C A T E B L A N C H E T T
H A I F A ■ ■ ■ A T L A S
■ ■ ■ F I L ■ E M O ■ ■ ■
M A R I L Y N M O N R O E
O W N ■ ■ D O C ■ ■ H A L
W E S T S I D E S T O R Y
■ ■ ■ U T A ■ E T H ■ ■ ■
D E B R A ■ ■ ■ A E R I E
D I O N N E W A R W I C K
A R N E ■ G A P ■ I S E E
Y E A R ■ G N U ■ Z E E S
```

ANSWERS

STAR APPEAL
(PAGE 160)

```
S W A G   A D A   T R O Y
E A R L   B A R   R E P O
T R I O   A T E   A D A M
A M E R I C A N I D O L
      I O U   A R I
C L E A N S   S A N D R A
O A K S         G O A L
W I G W A M   A R P E G E
      A G O   S A L
  A N N E H A T H A W A Y
S P A S   A I R   C A N A
K E N O   I D O   E C O L
I R A N   R E S   S O N E
```

A CERTAIN STYLE
(PAGE 166)

```
S L I T   P H D   T S A R
O U C H   R A W   H U M E
F L E E   A T E   E L O I
A U D R E Y H E P B U R N
      I R E   B E E
W I N G E R   S P A C E Y
E A C H         T I R E
E M O T E S   B O G A R T
      S O T   I O O
B R I T N E Y S P E A R S
T U T U   V A S   S H O T
U S A F   E L E   O S L O
S E R F   N E T   N O E L
```

THRILLERS
(PAGE 162)

```
L A M B   P D T   T R E K
I G O R   H E W   H A L O
S H O O   A P E   E V A N
A A R O N S P E L L I N G
      K A E   T E A
C A R E E R   S E S A M E
A B E S         T R A M
L U T H E R   B A C K U S
      I L E   E R A
A N G E L A B A S S E T T
B E L L   D O T   T Y R O
L A U D   E N T   L E O N
E L M S   R O Y   E D I E
```

TV TRIVIA
(PAGE 168)

```
H A D J   S P A   T I F F
A L O E   T O R   H O A R
R A N K   O U T   E T R E
T R A Y L O R H O W A R D
      L E G   U R I
L E E L E E   R A Z Z E D
A L T A         A A R E
P I C N I C   M O R G A N
      D O H   C O D
S O P H I E S C H O I C E
L O R Y   E T A   F A R E
I Z O D   S E I   I G O R
P E P E   E R N   D O P Y
```

WOMEN OF ACTION
(PAGE 164)

```
T O M B   B B S   J U T E
A D I A   R A T   U P O N
L E N T   U R E   L I D O
C R I M I N A L M I N D S
      A N C   L I E
C R U N C H   A C C R U E
S U R F         H A T S
I G L O O S   S T R E E P
      R C A   P O I
P A G E T B R E W S T E R
O L A V   R O E   T I L E
M O L E   E N D   I D E A
P E E R   S A O   E Y E D
```

LEADING AMYS
(PAGE 170)

```
S T O M P   S M U   A L L
L O R R E   K E G   M I A
A M Y I R V I N G   Y E T
T E X   S A M   A R G U E
      F I T   A M E R
T R A L A   U N S N A R L
L I M A   A M Y   A N T E
C A Y M A N S   O T T E R
      A B L E   S P A
C A D E T   L E A   P I T
I R A   A M Y A Q U I N O
T I M   R E L   U S U R Y
E D S   S T E   E A S E S
```

ANSWERS

SHIMMER AND SHINE
(PAGE 172)

O	W	E		S	E	A	L		A	H	M	E
R	A	T		E	L	L	E		P	E	A	L
B	R	A	C	E	L	E	T		P	A	N	S
S	P	L	A	T			T	I	E	D	Y	E
		B	O	O	P		N	A	B			
B	I	B	S		N	E	C	K	L	A	C	E
E	R	A		S	A	G	A	S		N	O	W
E	A	R	R	I	N	G	S		E	D	G	E
		R	U	T		Y	E	A	R			
P	R	E	S	E	T			V	I	S	T	A
O	A	T	H		B	R	O	O	C	H	E	S
M	I	T	E		A	U	D	I		E	L	I
P	L	E	D		R	E	E	D		A	L	S

DIET CONSCIOUS
(PAGE 174)

B	M	W		C	A	P		J	U	I	C	E
M	A	R		O	L	E		A	S	C	O	T
A	D	E		P	E	A		M	A	Y	B	E
J	E	N	N	Y	C	R	A	I	G			
	A	S	E	C		F	E	E	L	E	R	
		H	A	N	O	I		I	R	A		
M	E	D	I	T	E	R	R	A	N	E	A	N
I	T	A		H	Y	E	N	A		L		
L	A	M	A	R	R		Y	M	C	A		
		S	O	U	T	H	B	E	A	C	H	
C	A	R	P	S		R	I	O		W	O	O
A	B	A	C	I		E	N	D		E	R	R
V	E	G	A	N		S	T	Y		D	N	A

BUY BUY BUY
(PAGE 176)

C	P	A	S		A	P	B	S		J	U	T
H	O	B	O		Z	I	O	N		O	N	O
E	L	B	A		A	L	T	A	R	B	O	Y
F	O	R	M	A	L	L	O	G	I	C		
		I	C	E	A	X		P	O	O	H	
I	R	A		E	A	R		T	U	R	B	O
D	E	N	N	I	S	H	O	P	P	E	R	
E	A	T	I	T		E	O	N		S	Y	N
A	L	E	X		B	A	S	T	E			
		C	O	M	E	S	T	O	R	E	S	T
O	P	E	N	A	R	E	A		A	X	E	L
W	A	D		T	R	I	G		S	E	A	R
E	Y	E		S	A	N	E		E	S	P	N